.

THE ARRANGEMENT

Wayne McFall

authorHOUSE®

AuthorHouse™
1151 W. 2nd St
Bloomington IN 47403
www.authorhouse.com
Phone: 833-262-8899

Published by AuthorHouse 03/10/2026

ISBN: 978-1-4490-8917-7 (sc)
ISBN: 978-1-4490-8918-4 (hc)
ISBN: 978-1-4490-8916-0 (e)

Library of Congress Control Number: 2010902123

For Kay and Babe with thanks to Danny and mom

CHAPTER 1

The lone bare light bulb cast an eerie hue across the cobblestone floor of the old carriage house that had been converted into a four-car garage. The well-worn wooden door creaked open and a pair of red driving shoes padded past the boxy oil-embargo-era, crimson Lincoln Continental convertible to the first-generation scarlet Dodge Viper.

The morning was still cool so the man left the convertible top up as he opened the driver's side door and climbed into the car, setting his sack lunch and newspaper in the passenger side floorboard.

With a flick of the ignition the 10-cylinder engine throatily rumbled to life. The man's finger pressed the garage-door-opener button and the door opener hummed to itself as the door separated from the floor and climbed up out of the way over the man's head.

With a throbbing rumble the mighty Dodge eased out onto a 20-foot-diameter black-top plateau and rolled down the winding paved lane that led to the highway. At the bottom of the hill the man glanced at the gauges on the dash. Seeing that they had reached safe operating temperatures, he pointed the nose of the car onto the road and squeezed the accelerator. The car launched forward and was doing the posted speed limit of 70 MPH by the time the shifter was in fourth gear.

Between the growl of the wind battering the convertible top and the precision purring of the motor, along with the exhaust, he barely noticed a pair of headlights that appeared in his rear-view mirror until they were right on him. The lights flickered in his mirror, as he was about to downshift and punch the gas when the vehicle behind him eased out to pass, politely tapping the horn to make him aware.

A smirk crossed the man's face as the gearshift went down a gear, the RPM's on the tachometer jumped and the nose of his car dove into the still dark morning.

The man's smile froze after he shifted into fourth gear as the car, now beside him, did not disappear by the wayside. He glanced at the speedometer, and the needle stood at 100 MPH. The man pressed the gas and watched the needle approach 120 MPH. The other car stayed with him. He was prepared to shift when the other car boiled past him.

Shocked and surprised, the man shifted and stomped on the gas. The red missile hunkered down to the pavement and started to gain on the other car. At 135 MPH the man caught the other car and was about to return the polite horn-honk when, without any warning, the other car fell back behind the man in his lane. He shrugged and let off the accelerator, but it was too late.

Another set of headlights appeared from out of the dark, and on top of that car was a set of red and blue lights. A sick feeling, like he had just swallowed a rock, appeared in the man's chest and crashed to his tummy. He slammed his open hand on the leather-bound steering wheel in disgust as he applied the breaks and downshifted in preparation to pull over.

The first car coasted past him. He watched the taillights as they veered to the right and pulled into the gas station up ahead. The man came to a stop, and soon the Sheriff was standing at his door.

"Morning sir, where ya off to in such a hurry?"

"Work," the man answered. He handed the Sheriff his driver's license, insurance card, and a black leather folder. The Sheriff took everything and opened the folder. Inside there was a gold badge with the inscription "Honorary Deputy" and a badge number. The Sheriff nodded knowingly.

"How did you come about this sir?" he inquired politely.

"I provided bulletproof vests for Ellison County," the man explained.

"Now you understand these operate on a point basis?"

The man nodded. The Sheriff pulled out a hand-held computer and entered the amount of miles over the limit the man was driving, and the badge number. There was a pause, then he handed the man back the badge along with his license and insurance card.

"And you understand when your points are used up the badge is revoked?"

Again the man nodded.

"Thank you Mr. James, you have a nice day and drive careful," the Sheriff advised, as he turned and walked back to his cruiser.

Ian James smiled politely, nodded, and folded the leather booklet. He pressed his billfold into his back pocket. He glanced behind him, cranked the front wheels and pulled back out onto the road. Upon reaching the gas station he wheeled his car in, behind a familiar pair of taillights.

The other car, he discovered, was also red and sat at the forward pumps. The driver appeared to be sitting in the car, waiting as if it was a full-service island. Ian cut off the motor of the Viper, climbed out, and strolled up to the car. Under the well-lit canopy he could see the other car was a new Dodge Charger SRT-8. As he approached the driver's side, the power window eased down and a woman's hand reached out holding a credit card.

"Fill'er up," a smooth voice purred.

Trance-like, Ian took the card, which featured a vintage airplane, from the petite hand that had red fingernail polish and inserted it into the slot on the gas pump. He pulled the nozzle and squeezed the gallons into the tank until it was full. When he was finished he replaced the nozzle and stepped to the driver's door to return the card.

The window eased down and Ian found himself looking into the most beautiful doe-brown eyes he had ever seen, separated by a gentle round nose and flanked by straight brown hair. The woman's full red lips smiled easily at him.

"Thank you for taking the heat back there."

"How did you know?"

"Woman's intuition and a scanner wired into the radio, there's a whole other world out there," she explained, as she flicked her shoulder-length hair.

"Well, you owe me breakfast then," Ian informed her.

The woman glanced at the clock on the dashboard and spied the greasy spoon diner at the far end of the gas station lot.

"Alright," she answered good-naturedly and pointing at the diner, "it's a date."

She winked at him, rolled up the window, and pulled her car around to the diner, parking so it was facing the street. Ian, as was his practice, did likewise as he did not like backing into traffic. He had never seen a woman do that.

When he got out of the car, she was waiting for him. He walked up to her and they strode to the door. A neon sign proclaimed the diner's name was "Camille's". He pulled the door open for her and they stepped into a small lobby. A thin woman with bleached-blonde hair and crooked teeth approached them.

"This way," she ordered. Ian and the woman followed obediently to a small booth in the corner. The waitress slapped the dog-eared menus onto the worn smooth table, placed the two glasses of water from her tray onto napkins, and over her shoulder she said she would come back as she walked away.

Ian and the woman looked at each other and then at the retreating server. They each realized they did not know each other's names.

"My name is Ian, what's yours?" he asked, his hand extended as they were still standing at the table.

"Joanne," the woman answered, as she briefly squeezed his hand before they each made their way around the table; neither wanted to sit with their back to the door.

Silence.

She picked up the menu and scanned the selection. Ian did likewise, taking a swig of water as he surveyed the options.

"So, what'll it be?" the waitress boomed, startling the quiet couple.

Ian looked at Joanne and nodded for her to place her order.

"I'll take the sirloin breakfast platter," Joanne began.

"How do you want that cooked?" the waitress asked.

"Medium-well."

"Bacon or sausage?"

"Bacon."

"How do you want the eggs?"

"Scrambled."

"Toast or muffin?"

"Toast."

"White or wheat?"

"Wheat."

"And what do you want to drink with that?"

"Orange juice."

The waitress smiled politely then snapped up Joanne's menu.

"And you sir?" she inquired.

"The same please," Ian responded, as he folded the menu and handed it to the waitress. She hesitated for a moment, then took the menu, wrote a two next to Joanne's order, nodded and walked away.

Alone again with their waters, there was silence.

"So, where were you heading to in such a hurry?" Ian casually probed.

"To work, how about you?"

"Me too."

Silence.

"Where do you work?" Joanne asked, as she began to feel like she was on a blind date reality television show.

"I manage a distribution center," Ian explained, trying to make conversation. "It's a warehouse; there are 50 people working there I do payroll for."

Silence.

"Where do you work?" he asked.

"At the airport."

Silence.

"Like at a gate?"

"I'm a pilot."

"What do you fly?"

"Anything with wings."

Ian coughed unexpectedly.

"How long have you been flying?" he asked.

5

"Always," Joanne whispered, as she turned and looked at Ian. He had premature salt-and-pepper hair and full eyebrows. His hazel eyes flickered from the light cast from the lamp overhead. He had a Roman nose and thin lips that seemed to stay in a perpetual smirk, as if he was always ready to laugh.

The food arrived and they ate, talking little. Time had gotten away from them and they each had someplace where they needed to be. The check came and Ian paid the waitress before she could step away. The waitress thanked them, scooped up their empty plates, and was gone.

There was another awkward silence until Joanne pulled out her business card and slid it across the table. Ian picked it up and looked at the logo. There was a blue tail of an airplane, and on the tail was a gold "C" with a small lightning bolt inside. The name "Air Coryell" was printed on the center of the card, and "J. A. Brookfield" was at the bottom, along with a phone number and a website.

"Call me when you want to fly," Joanne said, as she stood up.

"What do you want me to call you?" he asked, smirking, as he too stood and looked evenly into her brown eyes.

"Anything but late for dinner," she stated.

"OK, how about dinner then, tomorrow?"

"What's on the menu?"

"Sirloin, medium-well, scrambled eggs, wheat toast, bacon, and orange juice."

"Oh, I drink grape juice for dinner," she chided him playfully.

"Grape juice it is then. Tomorrow night." He pulled out his business card and wrote his home phone number on the back and was about to provide directions to his home when she told him she had seen him pull out of his driveway, so she knew where he lived.

He nodded, remembering the strange circumstances that had brought them together. He waved to her and stepped into the bathroom to wash his hands. When he came out, she was gone.

He stepped out into the parking lot and the new red Dodge was not next to his red Dodge -- a pang of loneliness crept over him as the sun began to rise. He climbed into the Viper and pointed it toward the Interstate. If he was going to get groceries after work, he had better get to work to get things done.

Chapter 2

Ian was laying out silverware on the table when he heard a knock on the screen door. A warm smile spread across his face and his heart skipped a beat as he saw her on the porch of the rustic farmhouse. He strode to the door, pushing it open for her and handing her a stone goblet of grape juice.

"Service with a smile," he offered, with a grin.

"Are you trying to get me liquored up to stay the night? And here I thought you were a good guy."

"It's just grape juice," Ian sputtered innocently.

"That's alright, my overnight bag is in the car, this is closer to the airport for me. Mind if I stay? Ya got an extra room for the night?"

Flustered, Ian glanced down the hall. His sports memorabilia room did not have a bed and the other room had his weight set.

"Uh," he stammered.

"It's OK, I can sleep on the couch tonight." She took a swig of the grape juice, swallowed and gave him a peck on the cheek, vibrating her lips as a person would do on a baby's tummy.

Ian stepped back with his mouth open in surprise.

"I'm hungry too, when do we eat?" she asked with a sweet smile. She stepped to the table and stood at the chair, waiting for Ian to pull it out for her, glancing at him twice before he realized his obligation. She thanked him and sat down.

He opened a cupboard door and eased out two tan plates that featured ducks walking across the center.

"Ahhh, a momma, a daddy, and a baby, quite a family don't you think?"

"Uh, yea," Ian stammered, wondering if she was for real or not.

He brought the steaks over on a tray and placed one on each plate with tongs.

"Do you have a food handlers permit?" she inquired, with a serious look on her face.

"Uh, I had one in high school if that is OK," he explained.

"Oh good, a guy that has worked with people and can cook, that's extra points," she said waving her pointer finger in the air like a Styrofoam #1 hand at a ballgame.

He chuckled. "She is crazy," he thought.

"Yeah I'm crazy, and I'm good at it," she offered, as he brought the rest of the meal to the table.

They ate and got to know each other.

"So you have always flown?" he asked.

"Yeah, cause of my dad," she answered.

"Oh, where is he?"

"Arlington."

"Texas?"

"Cemetery."

"Oh, I'm sorry."

"It's OK, it's what he wanted."

"And your mom?"

"Retirement home in Minnesota, she's a mermaid so she likes to be by the water, the Land of 10,000 Lakes and all."

Ian looked up at her eyes. They were shiny and she was about to cry. He looked down at his plate as she dabbed a tear away with her napkin.

"She lost it when dad died, she can't take care of herself any more," Joanne whispered.

Silence.

"And you?" she asked.

"My parents are happily divorced and my mom plays Grandma for my sister's three children in the Ozarks," Ian shared.

"So it's just us then?" she asked, like a starlet in a disaster movie.

"Yep, just us," Ian responded as he sat up straight, "just us."

After the meal they sat down on the couch. She set her purse down on the floor and a dog-eared book slipped out onto the carpet.

Ian loved books, as his vast collection in the cabinets along the wall would attest. He scooped up the book and held it in his hands.

"'What Speed Looks Like' by race car driver Bobby Isaac," he read the book cover aloud, "Wow."

He handed the book back to her.

"Can I ask you something?" he requested, his voice quivering.

She nodded slightly and a little smile curled around her lips.

"Were you born a dude?" Ian whispered.

Her smile broadened and she began unbuttoning her sweater.

"Would you like to see the results of modern medicine?" she asked, in a smooth, even husky voice.

Ian did not know whether to jump off the couch or sit there politely while the person in front of him appeared ready to disrobe.

She flipped off the sweater to reveal her well-toned arms, a flat tummy, and a black sports bra.

"Wanna flip for it?" she asked as she stood up in front of him.

He stood up also. She reached her arms toward him so he politely returned the gesture. Their arms touched momentarily when suddenly his feet were pulled out from under him.

Then he was gasping for air as his back slammed to the floor and she was sitting on his hips, pressing his hands above his head into the carpet with her right hand and stroking his face with her left hand, the smile curling her lip again.

"First look is free, second one will cost you," she whispered as she leaned down and gave him a peck on the forehead.

Now he smiled.

"The question you have to ask yourself is 'Do you feel lucky?' Well do you?"

He hinged himself at the hips and lifted his leg up behind her.

With their eyes locked on each other, both with a smirk on their face Ian slipped his toe under her chin and suddenly pressed her back to the floor.

"I think what we have here is a failure to communicate," he quipped as he sat up and somewhat towered over her.

"We ain't fallin' for no banana in the tailpipe," she growled. She arched her back and rolled over, breaking his hold. They sat on the floor looking into each other's eyes and smiling. It was like they were looking at a gender mirror image of each other.

"You should not drink and bake," he breathed.

"Goodnight John Boy," she whispered as she gave him a peck on the cheek.

She got up from the floor and went outside to the car to get her overnight bag. He cleaned off the table and put the plates into the dishwasher as she slipped into the bathroom. When she came out he was back on the couch flipping through the book. It had many portions marked.

"Did you know him?" Ian asked.

"My dad did, they were pretty close." She gave him a peck on the cheek and snatched the book out of his hand. "Some people shoot and gamble," she whispered in his ear as she grasped his hand and pulled him up off the couch.

"Crazy," Ian muttered to himself as he walked to his bedroom. "Goodnight Mary Ellen," he whispered.

The next morning Ian awoke from his slumber to a whirring sound coming from the kitchen. He climbed out of bed and stumbled into the kitchen, where Joanne stood wearing a white blouse, black slacks and black shoes. Her hair was pulled neatly back.

"You are out of strawberries," she informed him, "oh, and ice cream."

He stepped over to the refrigerator and pulled it open. The strawberries were gone. Then he saw the empty container in the trash can. He looked over at her, she shrugged and smiled.

"What? Me worry?" she asked, as she took another swig from the blender. She wiped the milk mustache from her top lip and handed Ian a helping. He accepted, he tilted his head back and swallowed the chocolate and strawberry concoction. It was good.

"Gotta go," she explained as she floated around the front room collecting her things. "Thank you for everything."

"The bill is in the mail," he deadpanned.

"And the charges are declined. I gave this place some class, you should pay me."

"Easy Tigress."

"Meow," she purred. "To the Bat Cave!" She waved and was out the door.

Ian stood in the now empty kitchen and looked at the chocolate residue at the bottom of the blender. His house was quiet once more. Lifeless, dead. He had never had a woman spend the night in his home, and now she was gone.

He looked up at the wooden bookcase that lined the wall of the front room, thinking he might pull one of those books to reread, but none caught his fancy.

He walked back into the kitchen and rinsed out the blender. He fished the phone book out of the cabinet and called the bookstore to see if they had the Bobby Isaac's book. They did not have it but they could order it and they would have it for him in about a week.

He thanked the lady, marked the anticipated date of reception on his calendar, and set about getting his home back in order.

Days later he received an automated phone call from the bookstore, so he went down and made the purchase. Now he could know what she thought about.

On his way home he stopped by the grocery store and picked up some chocolate ice cream and strawberries to enjoy with the book. By week's end he had finished the tome and had made another visit to the grocery store to purchase ingredients to make the strawberry treat that was fast becoming a favorite of his. Sometimes he would add a lemon to give it some body.

He pulled out the business card she had given him, as he had used it for a bookmark. He turned on his computer and typed in the website. Blue and gold poured across the screen with the tail of an airplane, there was some general charter flight information, and the phone number.

He picked up the phone and dialed 10 of the 11 digits, lost his nerve and hung up. He looked at the website again.

"What? Is this high school?" he asked aloud. He picked up the phone and confidently punched the numbers. The phone rang.

"What!" a voice snapped on the other end.

"Hi, this is Ian," he explained, without trying to sound rattled.

"I know, and. . ." she pressed.

"How did you know?"

"Caller ID."

"Where are you?"

"On the runway in Seattle," she spit into the phone.

Silence.

"Did you check the website?" she demanded.

Silence.

"Did you read the book?" She wanted to know.

Silence.

"I knew it, just like all the others," she moaned.

"What?" Ian asked, in confusion.

"Stalker," she answered simply.

"I just. . ."

"Save it," she barked, cutting him off. "No, I cannot be your baby's momma, the sign on my womb says 'No vacancy', goodbye." The phone clicked and the line went dead.

Ian gently placed the handset back into the cradle. He wandered into the kitchen and his eyes fell on the blender, and he went to the refrigerator for strawberries and ice cream.

With the drink in hand he found himself in the front room where his eyes spied 'What Speed Looks Like'. He picked up the book and sat down at the end of the couch. He picked up a pen and made a note on one of the pages.

CHAPTER 3

A disjointed string of red and yellow leaves cut a windswept line across the weaving driveway as the rounded nose of the scarlet Dodge crept toward the garage that fall evening. With thoughts of work to be done on the 1990's Honda Del Sol acquired to compete in some local course racing, Ian hardly noticed the contents of the mail when he hauled the envelopes out of the box.

He laid the collection of brightly colored paper on the counter so he could prepare the chocolate and strawberry drink. When that was done he picked up the wad of envelopes and trooped to the couch to look them over. Some receipts, some contribution requests, a couple of newsletters and a packet.

He set it all aside but the packet. He turned it over and saw the "Air Coryell" logo. Surprised, he reached for the letter opener on the coffee table and slit the top open. He turned the packet over and a piece of gold paper fell out. He reached down and picked it up. Printed in the upper left hand corner was the "Air Coryell" logo, and beneath that was his name. Further down on the ticket was the flight information, Kansas City to Minneapolis, and the date of travel. He looked up at the calendar to check and make sure and realized the flight was the next morning. There was no return flight listed.

He turned the ticket over, then tapped it against his forehead, thinking. He stood up, walked over to the phone and punched in some numbers. It rang two times before a male voice answered. "Hello Chuck, this is Ian, something has come up and I'm not going to be able to make it to the softball game," he explained.

Chuck understood and said he would play in Ian's place. Ian thanked him, apologized, and hung up. Ian snatched up the newspaper as he strode into his bedroom to check the weather up North to know what to pack.

It was a cool crisp morning when the crimson Lincoln eased to a stop in the freshly lined parking lot that Air Coryell shared with two air cargo companies. Ian popped the trunk of the mammoth car and hoisted his leather suitcase from the expansive area that was big enough for its own zip code.

He pressed the trunk lid closed and made his way across the tarmac where the white airplane with the blue tail was parked. The guy on the fuel tank had just finished and gave Ian a casual wave as he pulled away, Ian nodded.

He set his suitcase down and it rolled over. Ian looked over and was surprised to see that the pilot had walked up behind him and Ian's suitcase had dropped onto the pilot's shiny black shoes.

"Sorry 'bout that, I didn't hear you walk up," Ian apologized.

The pilot nodded understandingly, pulled his hat down tight over his oversized sunglasses, and carried Ian's suitcase up the stairs and onto the plane. Ian followed obediently.

Once on the plane the pilot stowed the suitcase in the front galley and waved a hand to the light breakfast prepared on the table in the salon: a pitcher of orange juice, a box of donuts, and a tray of apples.

Ian sat down at the table and poured two glasses of orange juice as the pilot secured the door. A workman pushed the staircase away and gave the pilot the thumbs-up, the pilot returned the gesture and headed for the cockpit. When Ian offered the pilot a glass of orange juice, he nodded a familiar smile and stepped into the cockpit, closing the door behind him.

Ian paused momentarily, reviewing the pilot's face in his mind. The lips were quite full for a guy.

He returned to his seat as the plane was pushed out and headed toward the runway. An oddly husky voice came onto the intercom.

"We are cleared for take-off, please buckle up," the voice stated.

Ian did as he was told. The plane shot down the runway and launched into the pale blue Fall sky, banked hard right, climbed some and leveled off.

Ian had two donuts, quartered an apple, and finished his orange juice. He looked out the window but could only see great stretches of Iowa farmland beneath the clouds. He poured himself another orange juice. He stood up, approached the cockpit, and rapt smartly on the door three times.

He heard the bolt slide to unlock the door, and he held his juice carefully as he gently turned the handle and eased the door open.

There staring him in the face was a stub nose .38-caliber pistol held in the pilot's right hand while holding the yoke with his left hand. The gun silently motioned Ian to the co-pilot's seat. He immediately complied as he could not imagine what a bullet would do inside an airplane and did not want to find out.

The pilot looked over and smiled slightly, then pulled off the hat. The brown hair fell out from under the hat to the pilot's white shirt. The sunglasses were lowered to reveal a pair of doe-brown eyes.

"Fancy meeting you in a place like this," Joanne chirped. She extended her hand for the orange juice in Ian's hand.

"Are you stalking me?" Ian inquired, with a quizzical smirk.

"Do ya feel lucky? Well do ya punk?" Joanne whispered.

Ian looked at her. It had been months since he had seen her but he remembered everything about her, even the fresh scent of her shampoo. He was so glad to see her and wanted to give her a hug but decided against that, as they were thousands of feet off the ground.

She turned to him, a tear welled up in her eye and tumbled down her cheek. Ian leaned over and kissed the salty fluid away. Several more appeared and he rubbed his face and head up against her to absorb the stream of sadness.

She sobbed momentarily then cleared her throat and looked back out into the oncoming highway of puffy white clouds.

"My mom is going to die," she stated matter-of-factly.

"Why did you invite me?"

"Because you are the only one that ever asked about her." She took a drink of the orange juice and cleared her throat. "We will be there in a little while. Could you bring me an apple and two donuts?" Ian nodded, and went back to get the donuts and slice up the apple.

She thanked him between bites and said little else. Joanne was on the radio a couple of times, Ian lowered his left hand and held it out to her, and she grasped it without looking and squeezed.

When they reached Minneapolis she told him to return to the salon and prepare for landing. He went back to the cabin and buckled his seatbelt. Once they were on the ground Joanne pointed the nose of the plane to a white hanger at the far end of the airport and a guy directed her where to park.

When the engines were shut down, a guy rolled a staircase up to the door, Joanne popped the door open and gave the guy a friendly wave. He smiled and waved back.

Ian joined her at the door and they descended the stairs hand in hand, each carrying a small suitcase. The guy with the staircase nodded at Joanne and told her he would have the airplane fueled and ready to go upon their return. She thanked him and led Ian to a red Mustang with Minnesota license plates. He noticed the rectangular rental car decal on the window as she put his suitcase in the trunk. Joanne put hers in the back seat and they climbed into the car.

She pulled the key out of the console and slipped it into the ignition, the motor cranked over and rumbled to life. A smile crossed her face as she pulled out of the airport into traffic, all the while watching the temperature gauge until it reached the recommended level, then she pressed the accelerator and they left the traffic behind as they entered the two-lane highway.

She drove for an hour, then stopped for lunch. They repeated their orders they had from the first time they had eaten together – it seemed so long ago. This time there was a somber pall that hung over the meal.

Ian, sensing the reason for the trip, had worn a black outfit and tried not to chatter too much, but rather let Joanne talk about times she had visited and about her mom before she had moved up there.

Her parents, Joseph and Regina Brookfield, were in their mid forties when Joanne was born. He was often gone flying for the Air Force, and she was an Army nurse so there was little time to have a family.

When he had to eject from a flight due to mechanical failure, he broke his leg in two places. Ever the dutiful wife, she nursed him back to health, and somewhere along the way she became pregnant. He changed his commission so he could be with her. They ended up stationed in Florida, he trained the new pilots and she encouraged the young wives. Some of the young men's planes never returned.

From her earliest days Joseph would take Joanne to fly, and when she was old enough he gave her flying lessons – she was a natural. Since they were in Florida they met and became friends with some of the race car drivers. Life was good.

Then one day Joseph was asked to fly a vintage plane at an air show. He was familiar with the craft so he agreed. Once in the air, the engine chewed up a washer then burned out a bearing. Joseph saw the flames and headed back for the airfield, dropping fuel as he went. Upon reaching the airfield another plane was making an emergency landing. On a wing and a prayer Joseph made one more pass.

The limping craft was past its limit and crashed into a filling station at the end of the runway. A black plume of smoke signaled the end of the flight.

Her mother had to be physically restrained from running into the pillar of flames. The crash was on the news for three days as firefighters worked to put out the inferno.

Joanne joined the Navy as a seventeen-year-old with her mother, vacant-eyed, giving her permission. Shortly thereafter Regina resigned as a nurse and was transferred to Minnesota to be taken care of for her years of service.

Joanne threw herself into training and became an expert pilot and eventually applied to be part of the NASA program.

After fifteen years of military service Joanne got tired of the demands and decided to have her own flight service, calling it "Air Coryell", because her dad had always thought that that was a great name.

Now here she was making her final trip to Minnesota to see her mother. Before they left the diner Joanne went to the bathroom. She returned wearing a pair of black yoga pants and a red V-neck sweater. Her pilot uniform now folded up in her bag.

They climbed back into the car, she punched the address into the GPS unit on the dash and Ian drove. Fatigued, Joanne laid her head on his lap. She put a pillow on the console to support her neck as they got back onto the highway.

It had begun to drizzle when the red Mustang crested a hill and a massive buck was standing in the middle of the road. Ian jammed on the breaks and cranked the steering wheel hard left. The car swerved violently into the other lane and Ian could feel the rear tires breaking free from the pavement.

He let off the breaks and spun the wheel hard right. He heard a light thud against the passenger side and let the car spin around to a stop, facing the wrong way in the lane they had been traveling. Joanne had slammed into the dash and was then thrown back into her seat. A trickle of blood came from her nose, as her forehead above her eye began to swell.

"What's wrong?" she whimpered, coming out of a sleepy fog.

"A deer was in the road," Ian gasped, as his racing heart began to slow.

Joanne reached into her purse and snatched something out. She unlatched her door and leaped out onto the road.

"What's wrong with you!" she wailed at the buck as it still stood in the road, transfixed by the car's headlights.

"This is pavement where cars go!" she screamed, like a banshee.

The buck lowered his head, looking like he would charge at any moment.

"This is not good," Ian whispered to himself as he reached for the horn.

Joanne raised her arms. "Didn't your mother teach you anything Bambi? Was she there when you needed her the most!" she cried.

Her pistol barked and the buck leaped into the roadside foliage. She pulled the trigger until there was only clicking, then she slumped to her knees, sobbing on the yellow line in the center of the road.

"She wasn't there for you when you needed her most," she whimpered.

A screen door slammed from the farmhouse across the street. "What is all this racket!" a man's voice demanded.

"Call the Sheriff," a woman's voice chimed in.

"Not good at all," Ian growled. He raced from the car to Joanne's side as she sobbed. She was a pathetic mess.

He cajoled her into the passenger side and closed the door. He jumped into the driver's side, slamming the shifter into low and closing the door. The tires spun on the wet pavement and the car leaped forward, back the way they had come.

From around the next corner he heard two sirens coming from the direction they had just come from. He had guessed right about how close they were to town. He pulled over and turned the car around.

The two patrol cars arrived at the farmhouse, a man in overalls pointed in the direction the car had gone, and the first patrol car bolted off down the highway. The second patrol car parked in the driveway to take a report and recover the spent shell casings, as a lone red car crept past the impromptu crime scene.

The Sheriff waved the car by so he could set up a perimeter -- Ian waved at the Sheriff and continued on his way.

CHAPTER 4

At 4:07 pm the nose of the red Ford crept into the town of Normansburg.

"Population: 567," Ian observed aloud, reading the sign on the side of the road.

"Efficient, huh?"

Joanne was awake now, looking at the sights of the town she had visited many times. They passed Norm's barber shop on the left, Ian pressed the brake pedal and turned the wheel to the right when he saw the red, white and blue sign that proclaimed the location as Washington Heights Care Facility.

"Wow, a facility, no ambiguity there," Ian stated as the odd feeling he had inside began to mushroom.

Joanne shrugged and Ian stopped the car in the middle of the parking lot before backing into a corner spot. He got out, walked around, and opened Joanne's door.

She took his hand and they strolled up to what appeared to be the main house of a summer resort, with white columns and a marble floor entryway. Ian somewhat expected to be greeted by a goatee-adorned Southerner answering to the title "Colonel". There were two rocking chairs inhabited by elderly ladies chatting. They looked up and nodded.

One of them waved at Joanne, and she responded with the peace sign as she and Ian ascended the steps and made their way across the shiny hardwood floor to the front desk.

"Hello Ms. Brookfield," a square-shouldered man in a white uniform greeted Joanne, reaching out his hand with a warm smile.

She accepted his hand. "Hello Captain," she whispered back.

"Your mom is up front now," he explained as he led Ian and Joanne from the desk around the corner to Room One. They followed him to the door where he stopped and waved them into the dimly lit room. Two beds were inside. In the first bed laid a petite Regina Brookfield, a flower-print knee-length gown over her 98-pound frame, her short hair still surprisingly dark.

Joanne sat down on the edge of the bed. "Momma," she breathed as she stroked the old woman's hair.

"The Jo that was," Regina answered quietly. She opened her eyes and looked up at Joanne, then made eye contact with Ian. "We meet at last Mr. James," she stated evenly.

"Mrs. Brookfield," Ian answered with a nod. The old woman lifted her hand, Ian reached over and gently shook her hand.

"Good shake," she observed. "Mowed a few yards, huh?" she asked, as she lowered her hand back to the bed. He looked at his hands. "Calluses, they never go away," Regina stated.

"Yes ma'am," Ian answered, surprised at the woman's intuition. He looked down at Joanne. She had fallen asleep next to her mother, and Regina waved him off.

Ian nodded and strode quietly out of the room. He encountered the Captain at the desk. He was with a nurse and they were looking over a chart.

"Nice place you have here," Ian volunteered.

"Thank you," the Captain answered proudly. "We take the best care we can here, for America, you know." Ian nodded.

"Follow me," the Captain invited. Ian obeyed and the Captain politely gave him a brief tour of the facility.

Just as the Captain finished a buzzer started going off. Instinctively the Captain raced back to the desk, snatched a pistol from a drawer, and ran to Room One.

Two nurses and a doctor stood over Regina as Joanne groggily stood at the side of the bed and tried to keep her balance. A heart monitor had been wheeled to Regina's bedside. She had flatlined.

"She is DNR," Joanne wailed. Ian rushed to her side.

The Captain leveled the pistol at Joanne and Ian. "Nobody move," he ordered, as two muscled orderlies arrived in the room and drove Regina and her bed out the door, down the hall, and through a set of double doors.

"She is Do Not Resuscitate," Joanne wailed, to anyone who would listen. "What are you doing?"

The Captain turned back and looked them in the eye. "Taking care of her," he snapped.

Finally coming out of her sleep-induced fog, Joanne reached into her purse. Realizing what was about to happen, Ian tackled Joanne before she could pull out anything. He did not know if she had time to reload her gun and he did not want to find out.

"She is DNR," Joanne whined a couple more times. A whirring noise could be heard out behind the main house. Ian and Joanne made their way out to the marble porch and looked towards the back of the building, a black helicopter rose from behind a patch of trees and headed towards Minneapolis.

Ian and Joanne looked at each other and then back at the Captain, unsure of what they had just witnessed. The Captain walked up to them with a folded flag on top of a plastic case.

"These are her personal effects," he stated solemnly. "The United States thanks you for her service to this country. Good day." He handed over the case and the flag. Ian accepted them quietly.

With that the Captain turned on his heels and walked away. He strode back to the desk and picked up a telephone. He punched in a number with a Washington, D. C. area code.

"Music store," a woman's voice answered.

"The organs are on their way," the Captain stated.

"Very good Captain, you made bonus this month," the woman's voice purred.

"Thank you ma'am," the Captain responded before he hung up the receiver.

With the case in hand and a slumping Joanne on his arm, Ian made his way back to the Mustang. The sun cast its final light over the landscape and it began to feel like the day had lasted a week. He laid her in the front seat, then placed the flag along with the case in the trunk.

When the headlights cut into the dusk the world seemed like a lot quieter place than it had been hours before.

Joanne slept the whole way back to Minneapolis, so Ian kept the radio off and was alone with his thoughts. When they arrived back at the airport, Ian drove the car up to the runway. The plane was turned around, fueled and ready to go.

Ian gently cajoled Joanne awake and helped her up into the plane. He stood in the doorway as she methodically went through her pre-flight checklist.

When she was at last done she looked up at him and gave him a thumbs-up. "I got this," she offered.

"OK," he answered. He gave her a kiss on her cool cheek and stepped back to the seating area after closing the door. He sat down and unwrapped a sandwich he pulled from a cardboard box sitting on the table. He opened a package of chips and took a swig of soda. He would take Joanne her portion after they were off the ground.

The plane turned and headed toward the runway. Reaching the end the plane turned and was ready for take-off.

A minute went by and then another. Something was not right. Ian made his way back to the cockpit. It was locked. He pounded on the door.

"You alright Joanne?" he inquired.

No answer.

He hammered on the door again. He heard the lock slide over and he opened the door. Joanne looked up at him, her eyes glassy, the pistol on her lap.

"Momma's out there," she whispered, pointing at the runway. "She is calling me to come join her."

Ian snatched the microphone from its hanger. "Tower, this is Air Coryell, we have engine failure and need immediate assistance off the runway," he barked.

"Copy that Air Coryell," a tired voice from the tower answered. A tug rumbled down the runway as three planes now sat behind the blue-tailed airliner.

The tug arrived and pulled the plane back to the hangar. When they arrived Ian carried Joanne back to the Mustang and gently laid her in the back seat. She looked up at the upholstery. "I like the pony interior," she whispered before she drifted off to sleep.

Ian stowed their bags and the plastic case along with the flag in the trunk. He climbed into the front seat and pointed the car South toward home.

Two stops at gas stations and hours later the Mustang pulled into the winding lane that led to Ian's home. He carried Joanne inside, took off her shoes, and placed her in his bed under the covers. He brought in the contents of the trunk and fell asleep on the couch, exhausted.

The afternoon sun cut a swath through his front window, dancing across the glass on the coffee table, casting a reflection into his eyes. He awoke with a start and slowly remembered how the previous day had gone. He sat upright and rubbed his eyes. He was starving. He looked like roadkill. He glanced around the front room. The plastic case and her bag were nowhere to be found.

He raced to the bedroom. The bed was undisturbed, as if no one had slept there. He dropped to his knees and wrenched the covers back, sniffing the sheets to see if there was the faintest scent that she had been there. He thought he could smell something, but it might be fabric softener. He scrambled downstairs. There was a light circle of moisture on the floor where the washer had pushed out the water into the drain after the rinse cycle, as she had cleaned the bedding. He slammed his fist on the washer and then took the stairs two at a time to the front room to look out at the driveway. The Mustang was gone.

With a tightness of longing in his stomach he picked up the telephone and ordered a pizza to be delivered. By the time he got out of the shower the pizza had just arrived. He had ordered half for her and half for himself. He paid the driver and closed the door to eat alone.

CHAPTER 5

Halloween came and Ian put half a bale of hay and a scarecrow in his front yard. A family from down the road brought their children by, dressed up as characters from "The Wizard of Oz" and asked him if they could take some pictures. He said they could and he watched, interested, as the father was so gentle with the children.

With Ian's father having left their home when he was nine years old, Ian had missed out a lot on what it took to be a man. He watched fathers at church, baseball games, and the grocery store. He made mental notes on how he might possibly handle those situations if he were a dad. He did not want to write anything down. He felt if somebody were to find what he had written, it would appear he was a failure.

He went and visited his sister and her children for Thanksgiving in the Ozarks. He thought he was a good uncle, as he was faithful in sending birthday and Christmas cards with spending money enclosed. He was down to see them again for Christmas. For New Year's Eve, he attended a party downtown that featured a local band he had seen before.

Valentine's Day arrived and he was back to the Ozarks, this time to take his mother out to dinner. For Easter, he attended Sunrise Service at church and when April came, he was out to the ballpark for Opening Day. As usual the team had cobbled together a group of veteran ballplayers and rookies to see what would become of that.

Then there was the May Day Car Show. Cars from all over the Midwest would be there. He had taken home a Second Place trophy for the Viper and a Third Place with the Lincoln in previous years. This year, he tossed both key chains into a box and would take whichever he pulled out. He reached in and fished out the Viper keys. Good, it had a full tank of gas.

He padded down the steps, the garage door opened, and the Viper eased out into the morning sunlight, a good day for a show.

He snaked down the driveway to the road. From there it was not far to the Interstate. By then the engine was warm. He rocketed up the ramp, reaching 100 MPH at the top – amazing torque. He loved the feeling of absolute horsepower.

He backed off the throttle, occasionally glancing at the rear-view mirror in case any other cars would be on the way to the show. He encountered a Porsche and gave the driver the Speed Racer wave.

When he glanced in the mirror he saw something he had never seen before on the street. "No way," he gasped as the white shape began to grow in the mirror. As it got closer he could begin to hear it, then it was beside him. He could not help but glance over and see the word "Hemi" on the silver plate on the door.

"Awesome," he breathed.

White with an orange Scat Pack stripe around the rear wing, the 1969 Dodge Charger Daytona was a true piece of automobile memorabilia, as it was one of only 500 that were assembled. He casually glanced at the driver, as the cars were door-to-door. The driver, wearing oversized pilot sunglasses, gave him the "Peace" sign. He was about to do a double-take, but the car was past him. Minutes later he pulled up to the show.

He got his car registered and eased between a yellow Chevy Vega with a chrome, big-block motor sticking out of the hood and a reproduction Ford Model-T police car. After getting situated, he joked with the owner of the Ford that their two cars together on the side of the road would make a good poster. The Ford owner agreed.

Ian popped open his cooler, pulled out a soda and took a big swig. For May it was surprisingly warm. He settled into his chaise lounge chair and applied some suntan lotion to his arms.

"Snake bit are ya?" a female voice asked. He looked up from underneath his white Breast Cancer Awareness ball cap he was fond of wearing and realized he was looking at the driver of the Daytona. She had a long black rubber snake in her hands.

"Would ya like a mascot?" Joanne asked, with a smirk on her face. Ian dug his hand into the cooler and flipped her a soda. She saw it coming and let go of the snake. Ian jumped up to catch the falling snake, his momentum carrying him forward, and then his arms were around her hips.

"Fancy meeting you in a place like this," he drawled.

"Like déjà-vu all over again." She smiled and kissed him on the cheek.

"That feels good."

"The kiss?"

"No, your hand is cold from the cooler," she whispered. Their noses were close enough to touch. They stood there, looking into each other's souls. Hand in hand they walked around the show, pointing out favorite things about cars until they were to the Daytona. "This is the first one I have seen on pavement," Ian gushed. "I saw one on a trailer once."

"Do you mind if I touch it?" Ian continued.

"It's not an 'it', it's a 'she'," Joanne ribbed, good-naturedly.

"Of course," Ian blustered.

"My bad, what is her name?"

"Ellison," Joanne breathed.

"Ellison," Ian repeated. "Beautiful, like her mother."

"Ah shucks, you're making me blush, Sheriff," Joanne chuckled.

Ian looked into the cabin. "I heard the 4-speed – that is nice. Oh wow, 18,000 miles, that is probably the lowest miles of any of them."

"Probably," Joanne repeated. They walked back to the Viper and Ian dug out a bottled water from the cooler as the sun rose high in the sky.

The judges assembled at the front of the show and started handing out trophies. "And the Grand Prize, 'Best In Show', goes to Joanne Brookfield with the 1969 Dodge Charger Daytona." Joanne smiled and waved, then dragged Ian along with her to receive the award. Everybody cheered. Hand in hand, Ian and Joanne waved. They looked at each other and smiled. They were like the King and Queen with their Court.

They got together for a couple more car shows and a charity road rally with the Viper. Joanne was a natural navigator, while other contestants used GPS. They came in Third Place and their prize money was donated to a local crisis pregnancy center.

When Thanksgiving came, Ian invited Joanne to the Ozarks. She said she would see, but then a pro athlete chartered the plane for his family so she had to attend to that.

When Christmas came, she had a run to Puerto Rico to make. New Year's meant a trip to New York. So it was a surprise when she invited him to join one of her customers on a flight to Hawaii for Valentine's Day.

Ian arrived at the airport in the Lincoln with the temperatures in the 20's. He was standing on the stairs when the retirement home van pulled up. An ancient man with a fringe of white hair around his head lumbered out of the van and over to the stairs. Acting as the valet Ian took the codger's single suitcase. The man clasped a bouquet of pink flowers in his bony hands. Ian helped him up the stairs and within minutes, they were airborne.

The man sat at the table. He had an orange juice and ate three Long John donuts. "Doctor says I'm not supposed to eat these," he said to Ian. Ian nodded and smiled.

"Doctor died three years ago, I'm 89 years old and I'm gonna eat what I want." Ian nodded and smiled politely again, as he was not sure if he was the in-flight entertainment or not.

The man went and sat by the window for a while, watching the country slip away beneath the plane's fuselage. He gently stroked the flowers. He almost seemed to be counting them. A tear welled up in his eye and silently trickled down his worn face, hung on his jaw for a moment, then fell onto his tan sports jacket.

He looked down at the flowers, then over at Ian. "Ya married young man?"

"No sir," Ian responded.

"It's a good life," the old man offered. "Good to me anyway." Another tear trickled down his cheek and fell onto his collar. The first one must have cut a path to follow.

"How long were you married sir?" Ian inquired.

Two more tears fell this time. "Nine weeks and two days. She died on a Tuesday," he stated. "On a Tuesday," he whispered hoarsely.

"I'm sorry," Ian whispered.

"Thanks," the man nodded.

"Did you get married in Hawaii?" Ian asked, in hopes he could pep the man up.

"No, she always wanted to go. She didn't make it so I am going to take these to the beach for her, because I love her," he explained as he motioned towards the flowers. Several more tears came down his face and onto his collar. He sighed, leaned back against the headrest and dozed off to sleep.

Ian swallowed a lump in his throat and walked up to the cockpit. He knocked three times and Joanne unbolted the door. "Got a live one here," he stated as he pointed his thumb back to the sleeping man. She nodded as Ian stepped inside and pulled the door closed.

"He said he was married nine weeks," Ian shared.

Joanne nodded. It was silent in the cockpit. Ian cleared his throat. Joanne looked over at him, her eyebrows raised.

"I gotta go to the little boy's room," he gushed as he stood up and walked out, closing the cockpit door behind him. He heard the bolt slide back into place.

The man was still sleeping. Ian went to the bathroom, then laid down on one of the couches and dozed off to sleep.

The cabin shook and Ian sprang to his feet. He looked out the window and saw palm trees. He straightened himself up and gently nudged the man. The man fell out of the chair and hit his head on the floor with a dull thud. Joanne opened the cockpit door and saw the old man sprawled out on the floor.

"He's dead," Ian offered, as he had grabbed the man's wrist and could find no pulse.

"Master of the obvious, thanks for that. With insight like that you ought to be in a management position somewhere, oh, you are." Joanne spit out acidly.

Taken aback, Ian could only hold out his hands and shrug.

"Now Five-Oh is going to impound my plane for 24 hours, man!" she snapped.

Ian shrugged again and looked at the man on the floor. Then he looked up. "Well, we have 24 hours of fun in the sun," Ian offered.

"Yippee-Ki-Yea, and me without my swimsuit. I'll have to go in my nude!" Joanne proclaimed.

"We can buy a suit, they gotta sell 'em here."

Joanne considered that. "Alright, let's do this." She walked back into the cockpit and notified the tower, who in turn contacted the police. Moments later a squad car appeared. The detectives asked some questions and Ian and Joanne answered them as best they could. By then the coroner's station wagon had arrived.

Ian and Joanne caught a shuttle and rode to the terminal. Joanne headed straight for the gift shop, while Ian stood at the island of hotel courtesy phones to arrange lodging. He called every hotel and they were all booked solid. He looked across the street and saw an Army-Navy surplus store. He glanced back at the gift shop and saw that Joanne had three different purple swimsuits in her hands, and figured that he had some time.

He stepped up to a car rental counter and requested a Jeep. He sprinted out to the lot and climbed into the yellow box on wheels. He drove across the street to the store and found a camouflage tent, a gas-powered camp stove and two air mattresses. He drove next door to the hardware store and purchased a pump and a thin steel washer. He drove back across the street with his newly acquired booty.

Joanne walked out of the gift shop, having purchased all three suits and a candy bar. She was wearing one under her clothes and the other two were in a bag. Ian waved her down from the Jeep as he was parked in the front circle drive. She ambled over.

"Going my way?" she asked, with a smirk.

"Absolutely," he answered heartily. He drove them down the street to a grocery store. He ran inside and snapped up two bags of merchandise and stashed them in the back seat.

"Provisions, check," he said with a smile as he took off down the highway. After about five minutes the traffic thinned out and the road was reduced to two lanes. Ian spied a spot and wheeled the Jeep onto the beach.

"Do you think we can camp here?" Joanne asked in a concerned voice.

"Sure, this is like a picnic area," Ian responded, trying to quell her concerns. He unloaded the contents of the Jeep. He set up the tent, then filled the air mattresses. Next he sparked up the stove to get dinner ready. Joanne peeled off her clothes and slipped into the water to relax and bob around in the tides until the food was ready.

At dusk, their tummies full, they laid in the tent on separate air mattresses in silence. "Thank you Tarzan," Joanne eventually offered.

"You welcome, Jane," Ian answered. They laid there quietly for a long time listening to the throb of the waves pulsating against the sand. She thought she could hear his heart beating, then his breathing quickened. When he began to speak it sounded like a 12-year-old going through puberty. "Would you like to be my co-pilot from now on?" Ian asked shakily.

Joanne smirked in the dark tent. "Let him sweat", she thought to herself.

She waited. "How about you be my co-pilot?" she counter-offered.

"OK, done deal," he sputtered as he put the washer he had gotten at the hardware store on her finger by the light of the moon. They hugged and he kissed her. She rolled over. "I get my plane back tomorrow," she cooed before she dozed off to sleep.

They awakened the next day to rain. Joanne wanted Ian to pull the Jeep up next to the tent so she would not get wet. She sat in the front seat and played with the radio while Ian picked everything up. "You look like you took a shower," she observed, when he climbed into the Jeep.

"I did," he answered honestly. They took the Jeep back to the airport to drop Joanne off. Ian returned all the camping gear to the store and walked out with a wave of his hand. He returned the Jeep to the rental counter and caught the shuttle out to the plane where Joanne was doing her pre-flight checklist. He climbed the stairs and noticed the old man's flowers in a vase sitting on the table, along with donuts and orange juice.

"Those flowers were to go to the beach for that guy's wife," Ian explained.

"They are mine now," Joanne said with a shrug. "Finders keepers, losers weepers."

Ian's lip curled into a snarl. What had he gotten himself into, he wondered? He walked back and snatched one of the flowers from the vase and hailed a luggage truck. "Can you throw this onto the beach?" he asked the driver. The guy took the flower and nodded.

Joanne watched the exchange through the side window and rolled her eyes. She guided the plane out onto the runway and they jumped up into the sky.

CHAPTER 6

They had known each other two years and with each of them being in their late thirties, they figured it was time to settle down. They went and met Ian's mom for Easter, as well as his sister and her family. They all said she was charming.

They decided to get married on April 1st, because Joanne thought that would be clever and funny. Ian went along with the idea. For her bridesmaid, Joanne had an old friend from school to fill that role. Ian had heard her mention Betty before but had never met her. She was tall and thin with straight black hair and glasses. She smiled easily and tended to look down at the floor when she talked to people.

Ian had his nephew Arthur as his best man and his nieces, Claire and Marla, as flower girls. The ring bearer was the neighbor boy who had been in the "Wizard of Oz" picture.

The wedding took place outside at a local park on a sunny afternoon. Trained birds were released into the sky after the vows were exchanged. It was a beautiful ceremony. The following day Joanne had a charter to Puerto Rico, so that became the honeymoon, an overnight in San Juan. The next day they flew back, smirking at each other in the cockpit.

For the May Day Car Show, Ian wanted them to enter the Lincoln together. Joanne was not fond of the Lincoln, so she picked up a charter to Green Bay. Disappointed that her heart was not into it, he did not attend the show for the first time in five years. He received some e-mails saying that he was missed. He appreciated that.

When Joanne returned home that night he wanted to talk. She licked his ear and went to sleep. He was not fond of the ear licking, because he knew it was a stripper move, but she enjoyed doing it so he let her.

By their first anniversary Ian had talked Joanne into considering being a mom. She had virtually no interest in that at all. She finally relented so that he would get off of her case. She quit taking birth control. The arrangement was that Ian would be the primary caregiver, so she could continue to fly.

They attended the May Day Car Show with the Daytona and a photographer from a car magazine was there. He asked Joanne about letting him take pictures of the car for the magazine. She agreed, if her airplane could be in the background as a way to advertise. The photographer took down her contact information and said he would call.

A month later he was back in town and they met at the airport for the photo shoot. After the pictures were taken he invited her out for dinner and she accepted. He shared some of his stories of cars that he had photographed. After a while Joanne launched into talking about places she had flown and cars she had seen. The photographer politely paid for dinner and was on his way. The pictures of the car and a story appeared in the magazine two months later, and Joanne received five complimentary copies.

"The airplane was visible in only one picture," she complained, to anyone who would listen.

And then it happened. One morning on the way back from taking a well-known actor to the Betty Ford Clinic in California, as his life had spun out of control due to bad choices being made with a lot of money, she felt nauseous in the cockpit. At first she thought it was because she had not had a chance to eat breakfast. Then she looked over at the co-pilot's seat and saw the empty bag that had contained the breakfast she had eaten after all.

Suddenly her stomach wretched wildly and she vomited her breakfast back into the bag. Oddly appropriate, she thought, as she wiped her mouth with a napkin and tried to focus on getting the plane back to the airport. She landed, got the plane taken care of by the ground crew, and headed for home. She was shaky and clammy and felt disjointed and uncertain.

She pulled into the drugstore, which was not far from the house and purchased a pregnancy test. The teenage girl at the checkout counter gave her a knowing look. "For your daughter?" she asked.

"Excuse me?" Joanne answered.

"For your daughter," the checkout girl repeated. "Is that for your daughter?"

Joanne looked at the girl's nametag. "Listen here, Lori, it's for me, thank you," she snapped.

Humbled and embarrassed, Lori gave Joanne her change and silently turned to the next customer. "And how are you doing today?" she whispered to the next person in line.

"It takes all kinds," the older women answered, as she tilted her head toward Joanne as she left the building.

"Yep," Lori nodded and rolled her eyes.

The drive from the store seemed to take forever. Joanne pulled into the garage next to the Lincoln and climbed the steps into the kitchen, then walked down the hallway to the bathroom. She was there alone but closed the door and read the instructions on the box thoroughly, as she wanted to be accurate. Then she opened it up and read what was inside.

She did what the instructions said to do, washed her hands, and carried the test out to the front room to open the mail. She opened the front door and reached blindly into the mailbox. Her hand came down upon a thick 8 ½" x 11" envelope. She clasped it between her fingers and hauled it out of the box. A bill and a newsletter fell to her feet. She kicked them out of the entryway onto the carpet – she would look at them later.

The big white envelope had her name on it. Her eyes drifted up to the sender's name. "NASA" was printed boldly at the top. She dug her fingernail into the pull tab and ripped it open. A thick packet of paper was inside.

She laid the pregnancy test on the counter and looked at the cover letter, as that was more interesting to her.

"Dear Joanne, thank you for your interest in being involved in the Space Program. Your file has been reviewed and it has been determined you would make an excellent candidate for the program with your experience. Enclosed are the forms you will need to fill out and return to be one of the next-generation astronauts for this country."

Tears of glee sprinkled onto the cover letter, as Joanne ran the back of her hand over her face. She flipped through the application breathlessly. She could not wait to begin filling it out! Then one of the questions caught her eye. "Are you currently pregnant?" She had forgotten all about throwing up earlier. She looked down at the pregnancy test.

It was positive.

"NO!" she bellowed through the house. "Heck no!"

The telephone ringing cut into her pity party. She looked at the caller ID. It was Ian calling from work.

"What," she snapped when she picked up the phone.

"What's going on?" he asked casually.

"Nothing," she lied.

"Oh. You sound upset," he offered.

"If you are going to be critical I've got other things I can be doing," she grumbled.

"Oh, alright," Ian breathed. It was like walking on eggshells with her sometimes. He did not know which Joanne she was going to get -- David Banner, or The Hulk. This sounded like somewhere in between.

"Sorry," he whispered.

"Can I use the Lincoln? I need to go shopping."

"OK," Ian answered, surprised. She had never driven the car before.

Silence.

"See you tonight for dinner," she stated and hung up the phone. To her it seemed like there had been an explosion in the space-time continuum that had sucked all oxygen out of the room. Her knees buckled and she sagged to her knees, sobbing.

An hour later she had pulled herself together. She had spent half an hour running the application and the envelope through the paper shredder until it had overheated. She changed clothes into a baggy sweatshirt and sweatpants that did not match. She climbed into the Lincoln. "Good, a full tank of gas," she observed.

She drove out to Babies Are Us and started picking things up, virtually everything. The total price was just under $1,000. She pulled out their shared credit card and paid. A stockman helped her carry it all out to the car.

She drove home, emptied the car out and stacked everything in the front room. Then she picked up the phone and ordered a pizza to be delivered – she also put that on the credit card. She went into the kitchen and pulled the scissors out of the drawer, then walked into the bathroom to take one final look at herself. She returned to the cluttered front room and opened her purse. There on top was her cell phone. She headed to the bathroom and looked into the mirror again. She held up the phone and took several pictures of herself. She looked back through them and was satisfied.

She picked up the scissors and began cutting her hair, bits and pieces at first, then big gouges, until she was done. "You look terrible," she said to her reflection.

"And that is how I feel," the reflection responded. The doorbell rang, the pizza had arrived.

On the way down the driveway the pizza delivery driver passed a surprised Ian as he pulled in. He came through the garage and encountered the altered Joanne at the kitchen table, as she hungrily attacked a piece of pizza.

"I'm pregnant," she deadpanned. "Here is dinner. After that there is stuff in the front room for you to do."

Ian just stood there in shock with his mouth hanging open. "Why are you doing this?" he asked, after he got over his initial surprise.

"Because I can," she responded matter-of-factly. Then she took another bite of pizza. Ian looked the whole messy scene over for a couple minutes, shook his head, then reluctantly sat down and had a piece of pizza.

After two weeks Ian had moved all of his sports memorabilia out of the bedroom to the room downstairs. He repainted the bedroom a neutral color for a nursery. After painting he had moved all the clutter from the front room to the nursery. Joanne did not help at all, as she had charters to fly. She complained that the paint fumes made her nauseous, so she spent several nights at her one-room apartment she had in the hangar at the airport. Meanwhile, Ian took a week off from work.

When the house was back together Joanne returned. Ian was glad to have her home. She seemed distant, even in the evening when she was with him. Emotionally she might as well have been out on the couch. Ian thought that if he could love her enough, she would love him, but she always seemed to have a far-away look in her eye, like she was looking for something else.

CHAPTER 7

Sitting in the doctor's office she was already angry. Why had she agreed to the arrangement? She was seated on one of three flower-printed couches with five other women, all with various-sized baby bumps. "Ugg," she thought.

She had to pass a charter off to another pilot so she was out a fare for the appointment. She hoped the other pilot would return the favor and refer her to a paying customer one day. She looked out the window – that was where she wanted to be, out. Out of there.

"Mrs. Brookfield," the nurse called from the door, snapping Joanne back to her appointment.

"It's Ms. Brookfield," she stated to the nurse looking her in the eye. The nurse blinked and directed her to an examination room, then told her what to do. The doctor would be there shortly to see her.

She changed into the medical gown and already felt exploited. There was a soft knock at the door, then it opened and the doctor strode in, holding out his hand to introduce himself.

"How do you do, I am Dr. Clarke," he said with a pleasant smile, as he gently squeezed her hand in his soft fingers. He let go and adjusted his black frame glasses that matched his stylish jet-black hair. Suddenly this appointment was not as bad as Joanne had thought.

He asked her the standard questions and filled out a form. He told her what she should be doing and asked her what she had been doing. When she mentioned that she was a pilot, his brow furrowed. "Do you plan to continue to do that?" he asked.

"Oh yes, that is how I make a living," she explained.

"Well Mrs. Brookfield, you are having a baby here now, it's not like a dog that you can leave to its own devices."

"My husband will be the primary caregiver. That is the arrangement," Joanne stated flatly.

Dr. Clarke nervously adjusted his glasses again and ran his hand through his wavy hair. "Alright then, I would say that when you reach 28 weeks you will need to discontinue flying until the pregnancy is completed, then remain grounded for six to eight weeks until you are fully recovered.

"And do what in the meantime?" she snapped. "Bake cookies?"

"Whatever," the doctor responded, half-hearted. He gave her some booklets on what to be doing over the next months, and one on parenting skills. She flipped through the titles and looked up at him.

"So when do you want me to come back?" she asked softly.

"Check with the nurse," he said as he motioned towards the front desk with his hand. "She can take care of all of that for you," he explained as he disappeared out the door before it clicked closed behind him.

Joanne changed back into her maternity stretch jeans and ankle boots, then slipped back into her red V-neck sweater. She returned to the front desk and set her next appointment to see the doctor. She could hardly wait.

When she returned home, Ian was there. "What are you doing here?" she asked when she stepped into the kitchen.

"We are having dinner tonight," he stated slowly and purposely.

"Uh, yeah, and I'm hungry," she offered.

"We are having dinner for Mr. and Mrs. Boltz to ask them to be the baby's godparents," Ian explained.

"Oh, yeah, right. I thought that was next week."

"Next week is when we ask Mr. and Mrs. Cruz."

"Oh, right," she mumbled as she went to the front room and turned on the television.

"Aren't you going to change clothes?" Ian called from the kitchen.

"Why, what is wrong with this outfit?" she asked, as she walked back into the kitchen and struck a model pose.

"Well, for one thing, whenever you lean over, everybody can see everything you have. That V-neck shows it all."

"Fine," she grumbled, as she went to the bedroom to get a different top. Ian could hear her pulling open dresser drawers and slamming them shut. Eventually the noise stopped.

He looked up at the clock. The Boltz's would be there soon. He had warmed up the oven and now slipped in the bread with cheese sprinkled on top. That would make a good appetizer. Next he poured the mixture of boiled pasta into a bowl, then stirred in cheese, along with meat and beans to create what he liked to call pasta-chili-cheese.

With the mixing done, Joanne reappeared and she agreed to prepare the drinks when Ian asked.

The doorbell rang as she poured the last water and Ian pulled the cheese bread from the oven. Everything was on schedule. Joanne greeted the Boltz's and welcomed them. They were a couple old enough to be Ian and Joanne's grandparents. Rick and Barbra Boltz had attended Ian's church for years. Ian had learned a few Japanese words that Barbra had taught him, as she had met and married Rick when he was serving in the military in Japan.

Ian hugged Barbra and shook Rick's hand, then led them to the table where they sat down. Ian doled out the cheese bread, which they dipped into the heated marinara sauce located at the center of the table. Ian refilled their drinks, then served the pasta-chili-cheese. The Boltz's seemed to enjoy the mixture and accepted a second helping.

Ian cleared the table after the plates were empty and put out saucers with apple pie and ice cream. The Boltz's decided to share one between them.

When everyone was satisfied, Ian cleared the saucers and refilled the drinks. "The reason we invited you tonight," Ian explained, "is we would like to ask you if you would consider being our child's godparents."

The Boltz's looked at each other and Barbra began to cry. Rick looked down and wiped a tear from his eye. Ian and Joanne sat quietly surprised. Had they just lost a grandchild? They both wondered silently. Then Rick cleared his throat.

"We are humbled and honored that you would ask us," he answered, as he reached over to his wife without looking her way, and they clasped hands instinctively under the table. Ian noticed their special bond and hoped to someday have that type of relationship with Joanne.

"What specifically do you have in mind?" Rick wanted to know.

"Well," Ian breathed, "we want you to be part of the baby's life, like grandparents. My wife's parents are gone and my mom lives hours from here. We would like you to be token grandparents, be in contact a couple times a week to spend time with our child and teach them Japanese, along with birthdays and Christmas."

Barbra's eyes widened and she cried again. Rick patted her hand reassuringly.

"We would be delighted," he said with a smile. Ian and Joanne got up, went around the table and hugged both of them.

"That went well," Ian observed, after the Boltz's had departed.

"Yes it did," Joanne agreed.

"Good job husband." Ian smiled – she only said that when she was happy. He was glad she was happy.

The next week Mr. and Mrs. Cruz came to the house. Ian prepared the same meal and it went pretty much the same way. Antonio and Chela Cruz had grown up in Mexico, married, and moved to the United States where Antonio had built houses for many years with his own construction crew. Now retired, he tended to a large garden each year and doted on his grandchildren when they visited.

Ian asked if they could teach the baby Spanish and shared that the Boltz's had agreed to partner with them. The Cruz's accepted the request, hugs were exchanged, and this time Ian and Joanne cried as they began to appreciate how fortunate they were to have a community of folks to help them.

That night as Joanne drifted off to sleep in Ian's arms, he kissed her on the nose. "Pretty nose," he whispered. She laughed in her throat and was asleep.

CHAPTER 8

"Tower, this is Air Coryell requesting a runway and permission to land," Joanne spoke into the microphone as she approached the airport for final descent. With a plane load of drunken college students coming back from Spring Break it had been a quiet flight – the guys were passed out and the girls were asleep.

"Air Coryell, this is the Tower, you are clear to land." The voice gave her the coordinates.

"Copy that," Joanne responded as she brought the plane around and began the descent. She got below the cloud cover and was confused. How come she could not see the runway? It should be there. She glanced at the altimeter – she was low enough. She glanced back out the windshield – she could see roads and cars but no runway.

Frightened, she pulled back on the yoke and gained altitude. "Tower, this is Air Coryell. I am making a second pass," she explained.

"Air Coryell, this is the Tower, you are off course," a voice stated. He fed her the coordinates again and she made a second attempt. She broke through the cloud cover and this time all she could see was farmland.

She immediately pulled back the yoke and gained altitude. She came around again and picked up the microphone. "Tower. . ."

"Beep! Beep! Beep!" The screech of the fuel sensor cut through the cockpit and for the first time in a long time, Joanne felt a lightness in her chest.

"Tower, I think I am lost. Can you talk me in please?"

An older voice came over the speaker this time. "Air Coryell, this is the Tower, you are clear for landing." They had heard the fuel sensor go off also. The voice stayed on with Joanne and gave her step-by-step instructions to land the plane.

Within minutes the plane was safely on the ground. The stairs were rolled up to the plane, the college students awakened, and they lumbered groggily off the plane.

Joanne was still in the cockpit doing the post-flight checklist when she heard a knock on the door. She turned and was surprised to see the Junior Head of Air Traffic Control standing there.

"Hey Will, what's up?"

"Mind if I sit?" he asked. She motioned him to the co-pilot's seat.

"Kinda hairy up there huh?" he asked casually.

"Nah, I had it easy," she cooed.

Will looked down and cleared his throat. "Lou didn't think so," he whispered.

"I don't care what Lou thinks," Joanne snapped. "If all you want to do is be critical, I have other things to do."

"No you don't", Will said evenly.

Joanne glared menacingly at him.

"Lou called the FAA, you are grounded," he whispered.

Joanne's eyes flashed. "Heck No!" she barked, slamming down the logbook and stomping down the stairs. She stormed over to the tower and burst in, her eyes ablaze.

"Where's Lou!" she demanded. At first nobody said anything.

"He left," a voice in the back answered.

"Afraid of me huh," Joanne stated, strutting into the room with her blouse protruding around her waist. She was a laughable sight trying to play the tough guy.

"No," the voice in the back piped up again, "He just did not want to hear you whine," he said.

Joanne snorted like a bull and swore. The room was quiet as she glared at everyone and walked out, slamming the door behind her.

Hot angry tears trickled out of her eyes as she pulled her car out of the airport. She looked to the right and a sign caught her eye. It was a hookah smoking bar. She had heard about it from one of the ground crew guys. She slowed down and saw his car in the parking lot. She decided to stop in and check it out.

She wiped the tears away and walked into the dimly lit room. A jukebox played a familiar tune. She glanced around through the smoke and saw Hakeem seated at a table with two other guys. She walked over and sat down next to him.

"What's up Sweet Friend?" he asked, surprised to see her. He had invited her to stop by but had never expected to see her. He introduced her to his friends and they nodded.

"I had a rough day," she answered, leaning close so he could hear her.

"Ah, you come to the right place, let me set you up." He motioned to the bartender. "Set my Sweet Friend up will you, she has had a rough day." The bartender nodded and prepared her a mixture. He brought it out and set a smoking pipe of flavored tobacco in front of Joanne.

"I don't smoke," Joanne stated.

"Oh come on, it will make you feel better. Like this." He leaned forward to the mouthpiece and inhaled. His eyes opened slightly and he smiled as the smoke trickled out his lips.

"Now you try."

By now Joanne did not care anymore. She inhaled a big gulp and felt her throat burn.

"Too much, too much," Hakeem gasped, as his friends laughed at the inexperienced woman. Her head spinning, Joanne almost fell off the stool. Hakeem caught her and held her in his arms. She opened her eyes slightly and smiled. "I feel good," she whispered as the smoke eased out of her mouth.

"Me too," Hakeem responded, his hot breath warming her face. She smiled. He carried her limp body to a booth and she fell asleep on his shoulder. He patted her shoulder, then caressed her back. She was sound asleep.

He ran his fingers through her hair and kissed her forehead, followed by her cheek, then lightly on her lips. She gently kissed him back and opened her eyes. He kissed her firmly and she responded in kind.

"Hey!" a gruff voice growled. Through cloudy eyes Joanne looked up to see the bartender. "Get a room!" he snapped, and pointed toward the door.

"OK," Joanne whispered.

She felt herself stumbling toward the door with Hakeem holding her up, then one of his friends was helping her on her other side. She turned to say thanks and the friend gently kissed her.

Outside the cool fresh night air roused her from her fog. She stood up and pulled away from Hakeem and his friend. "Come on, we had a little fun," he said, putting his arm around her shoulder again.

She pulled away this time and made her way to her car. She collapsed into the front seat and laid her head back against the headrest. What had she been thinking, she asked herself?

After buckling her seatbelt she started up her car and pulled out of the parking lot to drive home. When she arrived she went straight to the bathroom to wash her hair and take a shower to get rid of the bar smell. When she had dried off, she took her clothes downstairs and washed a load of laundry. She climbed into bed, curled up next to Ian, and fell asleep.

CHAPTER 9

The day had finally arrived. Like an overdue flight that had gone through an electrical storm, friends and family wondered if they would actually hold their loved ones in their arms once again. Then the plane appears at the gate. There is unmitigated jubilation mixed with tears of joy, followed by gasps of relief and confessions to The Almighty that they would never take anything for granted again, ever.

The May Day Car Show had arrived and although Joanne felt as big as a house, she agreed to attend with Ian. They would take the Lincoln.

It had drizzled in the early morning and the sky was overcast, which made for a beautiful day. The birds sang and the motors rumbled. The temperature was perfect for human existence.

Ian and Joanne wheeled into the lot at 9:30. Joanne, with her oversized black sunglasses, felt like a movie star in a parade with people waving at her as the Lincoln crept down the row to their assigned spot. Out of the corner of her eye she saw some long pointy taillights. Somebody had brought a "Ghostbuster's" 1959 Cadillac ambulance. She thought that was funny.

When they were parked Ian pulled the chairs, cooler, and umbrella from the trunk. Joanne camped out on the chaise lounge and Ian faithfully applied suntan lotion to her neck, arms, and legs like an attentive servant to his queen.

After about an hour Joanne had a hunger pang. Ian opened the cooler and pulled out an energy bar and a juice box. A fellow pilot she had not seen in a while stopped by to chat. They talked at length about the proposed new runway at the airport.

When the pilot walked away Joanne had the sudden urge to use the bathroom. She was getting up to go when she collapsed on the pavement. She looked around and saw she was lying in a pool of fluid – her water had just broke and a sudden contraction doubled her over in pain. She yelped in anguish.

Ian raced around from the other side of the car to find her on the ground.

"We have main engine ignition," Joanne gasped. Her eyes rolled back in her head and she let out another cry of agony.

Ian gathered her in his arms and looked up as a crowd formed. He looked down at Joanne and her breathing had become very shallow. He looked up at the line of cars and saw the pointy taillights. "Who ya gonna call?" he whispered.

He noticed a child standing nearby wearing a white T-shirt with a ghost and a red circle around it. "Get your dad," he stated evenly. The boy's eyes widened as he turned around and cut through the crowd, yelling. "Daddy, daddy!"

"What?" the man asked when the boy ran up to him. The boy pointed at the crowd. The man ran up and cut through to find Ian holding Joanne in his arms.

"Who ya gonna call?" Ian asked the man, as he was also wearing the ghost shirt.

"Everybody get back and give this woman some air!" the man shouted. The crowd pulled back. The man reached into his pocket and pulled out a Cadillac keychain.

"I'm a doctor," he stated, then he flipped Ian the keys. Ian snagged them in the air and eased Joanne into the doctor's arms as he squatted next to her.

Ian ran over to the Cadillac. He yanked open the door, jammed the key into the ignition, and cranked the big motor to life. The crowd fell all the way back as Ian backed the Cadillac up to where the doctor had

Joanne. Someone grabbed the handle and the back door came open. The doctor gently lifted Joanne into the back. He stepped up into the back and slammed the door closed.

"Do the sirens work?" Ian shouted.

"Yes!" the doctor yelled back.

Ian flipped the switch and the siren started a mournful wail. The tires spun, the big ambulance launched out of the parking lot onto the street and roared away. Traffic cleared out of the way as they blew through light after light. "Turn here," the doctor ordered as the Cadillac's tires screeched in protest.

A few blocks and another turn. By now the doctor had called ahead on his cell phone and told the hospital they were on the way.

The emergency lane was clear when they arrived, and several medical attendants stood at the ready with a hospital gurney, like a pit crew ready to spring into action.

Ian wheeled the ancient metal into the emergency lane. Before he was stopped the door was yanked open and Joanne was on the gurney and into the hospital. The doctor was not far behind.

Ian jumped out, not sure what to do. A policeman appeared and told him to move the Cadillac into the parking lot. Ian got back in and did as he was told.

Once he was parked he went inside the hospital and started asking where his wife was located. He was sent to the maternity ward. When he showed up, he was told his daughter had been born and his wife was in recovery. He went to the nursery and a nurse walked in with a baby. She walked up to the window and showed him the armband. "Baby James" was printed on the piece of plastic wrapped around the tiny arm. A pink stocking cap was on her head.

"You have your mom's pretty nose," he whispered.

Half an hour later Joanne was rolled into a room and Ian sat down at her bedside. He looked at her as she laid there quietly. So beautiful, at peace with the world. He wondered who he would get when she woke up. He did not need to wonder.

CHAPTER 10

"I CAN NOT TAKE THIS CRYING ANYMORE!" Joanne bellowed. "How can something that small make so much noise!"

"She is your daughter," Ian whispered.

"Shut up!" she screamed. "She is your daughter!"

"She wants her mom," Ian pleaded, trying to hand the crying baby to Joanne. She glared briefly at the child, then took her stiffly into her arms. The baby stopped crying briefly and tried to nurse. They had tried unsuccessfully.

The baby began crying again, Joanne got up and shoved the infant into Ian's arms. She walked out of the front room through the screen door to the garage. She hit the garage door opener and stepped over to the Viper. She started the big motor, letting it warm up before she began to progressively rev it up. Its throaty roar soothed her inner turmoil.

After half an hour she came back inside the house. There was no more crying baby now, just the stench of dirty diapers and clothing ruined by being spit-up on.

She turned to the calendar and marked off another day closer to being able to fly again. If she could keep it together until then she would be alright.

Ian walked into the kitchen and gently wrapped his arms around her thin shoulders and kissed her nose. "Pretty nose," he whispered. She giggled in her throat, then tears trickled out of her eyes. "God shall wipe away all tears from their eyes," he softly sang as he kissed the tears away. Her breathing deepened as he kissed her neck. He picked her up and carried her to their bedroom, where he kissed her on the face. She moved her head slightly each time, indicating where she wanted him to place his lips. He did that until she fell asleep.

Rick and Barbra Boltz arrived one morning with a baby gift of a Japanese kimono. She whispered to the squirming little baby in Japanese. The baby looked into the woman's wrinkled face and smiled.

"What is her name?" Barbra asked, as she looked over at Ian.

"Maris Coryell," Ian responded. "It means winner."

"In what language?" Barbra asked.

"Mine," Ian explained. Joanne stood silently in the kitchen.

Barbra looked up at Joanne. "You have a beautiful daughter," she said with a smile. "Thank you for letting us be a part of her life." Joanne made brief eye contact long enough to nod, then she looked away.

Barbra looked down and whispered some more. Maris smiled and wiggled her hands and feet. Ian got up off the floor, walked into the kitchen, and wrapped his arms around Joanne.

An hour later the Boltz's said their goodbyes and departed after putting Maris to bed. Joanne sat down to watch some television, and Ian sat down next to her and stroked her ear.

"You have small ears," he whispered.

"My ears are normal-sized," she snapped. He continued to caress her.

The next day Antonio and Chela Cruz paid a visit. Chela spoke to Maris in Spanish and Maris smiled. Antonio opened a box that contained a white dress. Joanne stood silently in the kitchen – Ian went into the kitchen and held her close.

An hour later they left after laying Maris down to sleep. Joanne sat down on the couch to watch some television. Ian sat down next to the crib to watch Maris sleep. "You have small ears just like your mother," he whispered as he stroked her head.

The visits continued each week with the Boltz's and the Cruz's staying for an hour or so, sometimes feeding Maris and changing her diaper if needed. She was always happy receiving visitors.

Each day Joanne made another mark on the calendar. With a month to go, Joanne began accepting charter reservations. Her mood improved each day until the time finally arrived that she woke up, put on her pilot's uniform and prepared to drive to the airport.

Ian and Maris saw her off at the door. When she was gone the Boltz's arrived and Maris had a happy morning of play before a nap. The Boltz's departed and Ian sat by the crib to watch Maris sleep.

When Joanne returned that night, Ian had a light dinner prepared. Between bites Ian asked how the flight went, Joanne talked about how the ground crew in Milwaukee was slow as usual, and the bratty kids on the flight were unmanageable. She said their dad told her she was cute and gave her his business card.

"Did you accept it?" Ian inquired.

"Of course I did, I did not want to be rude," she said in a huff.

"Did he have a wedding ring?"

"Umm, I don't know, I didn't look," she answered before heading off to bed.

"Maris rolled over for the first time today," Ian said to the empty quiet kitchen. "I have it on videotape if you would like to see it. Oh, and you are welcome for dinner."

Silence.

He climbed into bed and kissed her on the nose. "Pretty nose," he whispered. She was sound asleep.

By Thanksgiving Ian had become quite the "Mr. Mom". Joanne had booked a charter with a local nursing home to take some widows and widowers to Branson for the day. That way they could rent a car and visit Ian's family so they could see Maris.

The flight arrived in mid-morning. Ian helped the aged passengers off the plane and down the stairs. After the passengers boarded a bus for a day trip to visit several of the singing venues, Ian, Joanne and Maris piled into a rented SUV and headed out of town for his sister's resort.

An hour later Ian wheeled the SUV through the gate of Selah Retreat camp and parked in front of the main house. The screen door exploded open as Claire and Marla raced to Ian to give him hugs as he exited the SUV.

"Where's the baby!" they cried.

"Easy there ladies," he answered calmly, as he opened the second door and unfastened the precious cargo. He took Maris in his arms and squatted down so the girls could see her.

"She is beautiful," the girls chirped as they gently kissed Maris on her hairy head.

"Thank you for saying so," Ian said with a smile. Joanne appeared from the other side and the girls each gave her a hug. She patted them both on the back as they all walked toward the house in the cool Fall air.

Ian led the way inside, nodded at his brother-in-law Rob Kerr, then Ian's sister Leah stepped out of the kitchen to give Ian a hug. She took Maris in her arms and kissed her on the forehead.

Joanne asked where the bathroom was and Ian knocked on his mom's open bedroom door. She stood up from her bed where she had been reading and gave him a hug.

"How was your trip?" she asked, as she squeezed.

"Good," he answered as he gave her a kiss on the cheek. Leah walked up to Ian's mom and held out Maris to her. Vera James gently took her newest grandchild into her arms and kissed her on the forehead.

"Dear sweet beautiful baby," she whispered.

Joanne walked into the room. "Hi Vera."

"Hi," Vera answered as she looked at Maris to kiss her again. A tear rolled down her cheek and she held Maris close.

They all made their way to the kitchen and Leah explained that Arthur had been invited by a gal friend to share Thanksgiving with her family.

Soon all the food was ready and the whole group sat down around the table. They joined hands and Rob said a prayer of thanks for the food.

The food was passed around and the discussion at the table ranged from the groups who had been hosted there lately to the children's schoolwork. From there it went to how far Maris could crawl to what she had gotten into. Occasionally Joanne would toss in a comment about a flight she had taken or a movie she had seen a preview for.

After the meal Leah and Ian cleared the table, Vera checked on Maris sleeping in her bedroom while Claire and Marla went to their bedroom to play video games. Joanne joined Rob in the family room to watch some television. Eventually everybody filtered into the family room, as was family tradition, to watch a movie together.

When the movie was over Rob had fallen asleep in Leah's lap and Joanne was asleep against Ian's shoulder. Vera had gone to check on Maris again and she had not come back.

Ian slipped away from Joanne and found his mother in her bedroom changing Maris' diaper. "There, all better," Vera clapped as Maris giggled. Ian walked up behind his mother and laid his head on her shoulder.

"Is it time to go?" she asked her son. He nodded silently.

"Alright," she breathed. She packed up the baby bag and carried Maris out to the SUV to lash her in. Ian roused Joanne from her slumber and thanked Leah with a hug. Ian carried Joanne out to the SUV and buckled her into the front seat. He hugged his mom and climbed into the SUV. He made a final wave out the side window and pulled out of the gate onto the road to return to the airport.

When they arrived Joanne was awake and ready to fly. The tour bus showed up, the senior citizens filed onto the plane with Ian's help, and the plane was rolling down the runway on schedule.

When the plane landed they were a little early. The nursing home bus was not there yet so the elderly folks cooed over Maris until the bus showed up as she had awakened. Then they filed off the plane.

The ground crew appeared to refuel the plane – two of them waved at Joanne and she waved. Ian secured Maris in the back of the SRT-8, as Joanne dozed off in the front seat. When they arrived home, Ian put Maris to bed, then carried Joanne to bed. She had to get up the next day and fly a family to Chicago for Christmas shopping on Black Friday.

After Joanne left the next morning, Ian bundled up Maris and took her along as he went out and purchased her first Christmas tree. When he had made the selection, he stuck the tree in the trunk of the Lincoln. They drove home and he put up the tree. He located the Christmas decorations in the basement and went about trimming the tree. He played an Elvis Christmas CD.

He had Maris in bed by 8:00pm and sat down on the couch with a hot chocolate to grade his handiwork when he heard the garage door opening. Joanne climbed the steps to the kitchen and collapsed onto the couch next to Ian. She was asleep in seconds.

"Merry Christmas," he whispered. He closed his eyes for a minute so he could prepare to carry her to bed.

When he opened his eyes it was daylight. He could feel a sudden tightening in his chest as he slipped out from underneath Joanne to check her logbook. He breathed a sigh of relief when he discovered a blank page for the day. He heard Maris stirring in her room and went to take care of her.

CHAPTER 11

FLASH. . .FLASH. . .FLASH.

Maris flinched -- the light that had flashed in her eyes was bright so she had to turn away. "Is that too much Babe?" her father's voice asked. She looked in the direction that the voice was coming from.

"I'm sorry Babe," he whispered as he kissed her forehead. Ian sat Maris back down on the floor, as she was transfixed by the blinking lights on the Christmas tree.

Meanwhile Joanne stood up off the stool that they all three had been sitting on for their first family Christmas picture. She strode back to the bedroom to change clothes.

Ian flipped through the envelopes he had addressed to see how many copies of the picture he would need to get printed. "Should we send one to the place that took care of your mom?" Ian called out.

"NO," Joanne shot back as she stormed into the front room. "Did you make out a card?"

Ian held up an envelope, Joanne snatched it out of his hand and tore it into small pieces, then she threw them into the trash can. She returned to the bedroom and threw herself onto the bed. Ian waited until he could not hear the bed springs bouncing anymore then took Maris in his arms and set her on his lap so they could enjoy the Christmas tree together. He stroked her ears until she fell asleep, then laid her in her bed.

He put stamps on the envelopes, climbed into bed with Joanne and went to sleep.

Virtually each day as Christmas drew closer Joanne had a flight to make and sometimes two flights. Ian spoke to her about them starting a Christmas family tradition. She kept putting off a decision, as she wanted to be available for possible flights.

With a week to go Ian relaxed and decided to accept whatever was going to happen. Then she had a cancellation the day before Christmas Eve. She was nearly exhausted.

For Christmas Eve he made hot chocolate and Joanne joined he and Maris in the front room as he read the Christmas story from the Bible. Later he put Maris to bed while singing "Silent Night" to her. He slipped into bed with Joanne and thanked her for being there. She nodded and went to sleep.

For Christmas Day Ian made a brunch to eat, then he helped Maris open her gifts. A nap followed and when she woke up later, they played with her new toys before going to bed in the evening.

Joanne left early the next morning to return passengers to their homes. Ian, with Maris in tow, hit the post-Christmas sales. When he returned home his mom had left a message to call her. He fed Maris and laid her down for a nap, then called his mom. They talked about how Maris' first Christmas had turned out. Ian looked forward to the New Year and Maris walking soon. Within the year she would begin speaking three languages. Raising her was his number one priority. He was even considering home schooling her for a couple of years and teaching her the basics, maybe even taking her on some field trips.

His mom listened carefully to her son and could tell things were not going as well as they could go. She kept that to herself.

For Valentine's Day Joanne had a charter to Hawaii. She did not invite Ian and Maris this time, so he had called a member of the ground crew at the airport and had him put a heart-shaped box of chocolates in her seat. She smiled when she discovered the box and called Ian to thank him. He was happy to hear from her that she appreciated the gesture.

"My name is Maris
I am the fairest
Of them all
My name will never fall."

Ian smiled at his daughter after singing to her. She stood up in her crib. "Happy Birthday Baby, you are a year old today."

Maris laughed and Ian scooped her up in his arms. "Everyone will want to see the birthday girl." He put a short-sleeved sundress on her and pulled a bucket hat out of her closet for her to wear. "And look here," he said as he pulled a plastic sack out of his pocket. He opened it up to reveal a pair of small sunglasses – "We have to protect the peepers."

He popped open the cap of the suntan lotion and rubbed some of the fluid onto her soft face. He squeezed out another dose and slathered it over her neck, shoulders and arms. She giggled and playfully danced around after he was done.

"Ya ready?" Joanne grunted, poking her head in the doorway. She really did not want to return to the scene of one of her most embarrassing moments in her life. But she knew the folks at the May Day Car Show would want to see Maris so she had agreed to attend, but this time they would take the Daytona.

Upon their arrival there was the usual buzz when the big Dodge with the race car-inspired bullet nose showed up. Once that passed there was the additional interest of the folks that wanted to see Maris. When Ian unbuckled her from her car seat there was a round of applause. Some people had brought gifts. A couple people congratulated Joanne.

After Joanne checked in she walked the cars with Ian as he carried Maris. When they had made the loop Ian pulled the chaise lounge chair out of the trunk for Joanne and reapplied the suntan lotion to Maris.

At the end of the show everyone gathered in front of the stage where the Master of Ceremonies led the crowd in singing "Happy Birthday" to Maris before the trophies were handed out.

"Pretty good birthday party huh?" Ian asked Joanne on the way home.

"Yep." She said little else on the way home. She climbed into bed shortly after dinner as Ian put Maris to sleep.

"Happy birthday," he whispered as she drifted off.

Waiting to turn out of the grocery store Ian punched the gas pedal and the big Lincoln lunged out of the opening and squeezed into traffic. A mile down the road he turned and headed to the Boltz home to pick up Maris, as they were taking care of her while he was shopping. He pulled into their driveway, got out of the car, and knocked on their front door. Barbra pulled the door open and excitedly invited Ian inside. He obediently followed her to the front room where Maris was playing with a toy on the carpet.

Barbra said something in Japanese, Maris looked up at Barbra and responded with two words.

"Yes!" Ian growled as he pumped his fist in the air. It was the first time he had heard his daughter speak in Japanese. All the trips back and forth over the months were starting to pay off. He turned and gave Barbra a warm thankful hug. He stepped forward and shook Rick's hand. Maris looked up and raised her arms to Ian for him to pick her up.

"Big girl," he whispered.

"Big girl," she repeated back to him. He talked to her about how they would tell Joanne when she came home that night. She smiled.

He thanked the Boltz's again and carried Maris out to the car. He drove home and brought her inside, then he brought in the groceries.

He had just finished putting everything away and Joanne showed up in the kitchen.

"Our daughter spoke Japanese today," he gushed.

"Oh, what did she say?" Joanne inquired as she pulled some juice from the refrigerator."

"I don't know, it was Japanese."

"Well, that's a problem," Joanne observed after she took a drink. "Hey, if she does learn Japanese or Spanish maybe she could help with the passengers."

Ian slowly shook his head. He could not believe that she was considering using her own daughter as part of her business.

"She could really help me," Joanne stated as her eyes lit up. She turned to Ian. "What was that about homeschooling you were thinking about? She could fly with me and learn.

Ian's jaw tightened. He could not believe what he was hearing.

"Where is she?" Joanne asked, taking a newfound interest in Maris. She strode to where Maris was in her bedroom. "How is mommy's girl doing?"

"Mommy," Maris repeated.

"Big girl," Joanne said as she squatted down in front of her.

"Big girl," Maris repeated.

Joanne lifted her up and held her close. Standing at the door this was the first time Ian could remember Joanne showing any interest in their daughter, and it was because she could possibly help Joanne. Ian felt like his stomach was going to wretch.

As the weekly visits continued with the Boltz's and the Cruz's, Maris began speaking more Japanese and Spanish. The Thanksgiving visit to the Ozarks was highlighted by what Maris was learning. Everybody was amazed by the little girl's intelligence.

The next day they all three went out and selected a Christmas tree. It was a nice family afternoon. They repeated what they had done the previous year for Christmas with reading the Christmas story from the Bible and they watched some video from their first Christmas. They were both taken with how much Maris had grown in the past year.

They had a nice family Christmas with a meal and Maris unwrapped her own gifts. Ian shot video and added it to the previous Christmas video.

Chapter 12

"Can I hang my cross?" Maris asked, as she and Ian stood back and looked at the Christmas tree the following year. Ian lifted the little wooden cross with green and red ribbon nailed to it from out of the decoration box and handed it to Maris as he smiled.

"Why is it my cross?" she asked. "I forgot."

"I cut it from the trunk of your first Christmas tree," Ian explained as she found a spot on the tree to hang the ornament.

"That's a good place," Ian offered.

For her fourth birthday Ian and Maris attended the May Day Car Show with the Lincoln. After they arrived Maris was surprised to see Ian pull a plastic battery-powered Mustang out of the trunk that she could use to drive around the show and look at the cars as Ian walked. Joanne had a charter and was not able to join them.

Ian pointed out little things he liked about each car to her. By the end of the show she had gotten very good at maneuvering the plastic car around.

When they went to the show for her fifth birthday Ian gave Maris a tablet along with a pencil and had her write down the engine's cubic inches she saw on the fenders so she could work on writing her numbers. She already knew what the word "Continental" looked like, so they worked on sounding out some of the other cars' names written in metal. She thought some of them sounded funny and she laughed at them.

Joanne had not felt well, so she had stayed home. When they returned to the house Maris raced into the bedroom to share with Joanne all she had written.

"And look at these," Maris said proudly as she held up some additional pieces of paper. "Some people let me do a rubbing of emblems on their cars."

Joanne looked at the childish scribbles. "That's nice," she observed, as Maris handed them over.

Ian had decided he would work with Maris for as long as he felt he could teach her as much as she needed to know. He purchased books about what a child should know and checked with the school district to make sure what he was doing was alright. He got involved with a local home school organization so that Maris could interact with other children.

He took her on field trips to museums and historical sights. He had her take notes on what they saw and then write a report about the experience.

One Spring Joanne flew them to Florida to see some Spring Training baseball games and visit Disney World. They stopped in to see her friend Betty while they were there. Another time they flew on a commercial flight to California to see a television show be filmed, and then they hung out on the beach the next afternoon.

They visited the state capital via the train for the state history portion of her education. They participated in a protest march in Washington, D. C. so she could see what was involved with the right to petition the government. While they were there, they visited Arlington National Cemetery to put flowers on Joseph Brookfield's grave and see the changing of the guard at the Tomb of the Unknown Soldier. Maris cried at the solemness of it all.

One summer Maris went with Barbra Boltz to Japan for two weeks of language study as they stayed with Barbra's sister in her home outside of Tokyo. She was becoming a well-rounded young lady.

Sometimes she would fly with Joanne on a charter. Ian's mom had made Maris a flight attendant uniform one Christmas and she loved it. She would serve the passengers and demonstrate the safety procedures like she had seen when she had flown commercial.

It was on a return trip home that Maris was sitting at the table writing when she felt the plane shudder. She looked up and around. Then she looked out the window. Smoke was billowing out of the left wing.

Meanwhile, Joanne felt the shudder and looked at the gauges. The temperature had climbed dangerously high on the left engine. She glanced over and saw smoke pouring out, so she cut the fuel off and waited. The smoke dwindled to a stream and disappeared.

"Tower, this is Air Coryell," she barked into the microphone, "I just lost my left engine."

"This is the Tower, what is your status?"

"I don't know, I'm not a mechanic, the engine just blew up or something."

"What is the condition of your other engine?"

Joanne looked over the gauges and they all read normal. "Fine, I think I can make it."

"Tower out."

She looked out at the horizon. At this altitude she felt she could see forever, like heaven. She remained at that height to give herself as much time as she could, in case she had to ditch the airplane, which she did not want to have to do.

She picked up the microphone. "Could I have the flight attendant to the cockpit please?" she asked softly.

She put down the microphone and something caught her eye. She glanced to her right and saw a string of birds. In almost slow motion they blew past her. She heard a grinding noise and then silence, as the right engine cut out due to a bird strike.

Maris pulled open the door. Joanne snapped around and made eye contact with her daughter. "Hold up your hands!" she barked.

Wide-eyed Maris raised her hands. Joanne reached behind the co-pilot seat and wrenched out a black backpack. She slammed it down over Maris' shoulders and snapped a connector around her hips.

"What's wrong!" Maris gasped. Joanne jumped out of her seat and shoved Maris back into the cabin. She reached for the door and cranked it open. Maris opened her mouth and nothing came out. Joanne pressed a button that was on the mechanism strapped to Maris' chest. "That is a GPS so your dad can find you," she explained.

"No," Maris gasped.

"I'm your mother, you do what I tell you to do. Do you understand me!" Joanne snarled. Tears trickled down Maris' face as she nodded. Joanne grabbed the strap on Maris' back and chucked her out the door. She heard Maris scream and walked away from the door back to the cockpit.

She sat down and buckled herself in. She glanced over to the co-pilot seat and the Grim Reaper gave her a friendly wave with his bony fingers. A pale hand from behind reached forward between the seats and rested momentarily on Death's shoulder, then the hand jerked Death out of the cockpit. A slim man stepped forward and sat down in the co-pilot seat.

"Daddy!" Joanne squealed in delight. The man nodded and pointed at the dash.

Joanne looked at the gauges and tried to restart the engines.

CHAPTER 13

The yellow school bus loaded with high school students lumbered into the Community Airport. They were there to see an example of a World War II fighter plane, as they had been studying that era in class. They were all talking and glad to be out of school for the afternoon.

Eugene Gregg could hardly wait for the noisy kids to get off the bus so he could take another pull from his flask he had under the seat.

The engine sputtered to life and died. It sputtered, ran, and died again. "This is Air Coryell, I need a place to land now!" Joanne shouted into the microphone.

"This is the Tower, you are clear to land at the Community Airport. They are ready for you."

A red fire truck pulled up to the runway at the Community Airport to provide any help. Three police cars raced onto the property and parked in a perimeter around the runway. Joanne hit the button over and over, trying to get either engine to come back to life. Then the left one sputtered again and came on. "Yes!" she screamed. She pulled back on the yoke and gained some altitude and control of the plane. The runway was in sight.

The engine sputtered and died again.

The fire truck was blocking his view so Eugene pulled the bus up past the fire truck to see where the plane they had come to see was located.

"NOOO!" Joanne screamed. The front landing gear slit through the top of the bus like a can opener. The rest of the plane slammed into the side of the bus, disintegrating the windows into a shower of flying glass. Most of the students were slaughtered in a moment. Those near the front of the bus missed the direct impact. They were spared with their lives and their cries rang out across the runway.

Mark Tibbits ran full-speed from his police cruiser to the demolished bus. He found the driver sitting in his seat in stunned disbelief at the carnage around him he had caused. The driver reached down to pick up a chard of glass to run across his throat when he was suddenly knocked back against his seat, his head slamming against some glass that had not been shattered by the impact.

"You have the right to remain silent!" Mark yelled at the chubby, unshaven man who smelled of alcohol that he was perched upon. Eugene gazed glassy-eyed.

Captain Ed Palmer arrived at the bus and climbed up the stairs. When he saw the driver pinned under Mark he pulled out his service weapon and pointed it at the driver.

"Please no, Captain. Not this way," Mark begged.

Captain Palmer pulled the trigger and shot out one of the remaining panes of glass on the bus. Eugene wet himself and began to sob uncontrollably.

There was a tremendous impact when the plane collided with the bus. The plane actually bounced up and crashed to the pavement an additional 50 feet down the runway. With the landing gear sheared off, the plane slid down the runway and rolled over. A wing broke off and ripped down the fence at the far end of the field.

The fire truck leaped into action, chasing the destroyed plane through the smoke and debris. When the truck reached the wreckage, six uniformed firefighters jumped out, two with a hose, and four others jumped up onto the tattered fuselage with the Jaws of Life.

Minutes later they had wrenched the plane open and removed a battered female victim. An ambulance rolled up and the patient was loaded aboard. The doors were closed and the ambulance took out of the airport with the sirens blaring.

Maris gasped for air. She could not breathe. She wanted to cry out, but nothing happened. Her head began to hurt and she felt like she was going to pass out. The fall was worse than any amusement park ride.

The mechanism on her chest beeped and the parachute deployed, as Joanne had set it to automatic based on Maris' weight. She sniffled as she drifted near a wooded area and crashed to the ground and pain shot through her ankle.

She laid there for several minutes, looking up at the sky she had just fallen from. She did not know where she was. She sat up and looked around. She tried to stand and immediately fell to the ground in anguish. She was not walking out of this.

Frustrated, she dug her hand into the small pouch she found on one strap and felt a bulge. She dug it out and found it was a cell phone. She flipped it open and found her dad's name at the top of the call list. She hit "speed dial" and the phone rang once, twice, then three times.

"Hello," Ian answered.

"Daddy," Maris whimpered.

"Is that you Maris?"

"Yes Daddy," she cried.

"What's wrong?"

"Mommy threw me out of the plane."

"WHAT! Why?"

"I think it went down," she blubbered.

Ian raced to the television and turned it on. "Oh no," he gasped. On the screen was a helicopter view hovering above the Community Airport showing an unbelievable scene of destruction and carnage of the demolished airplane and a virtually indistinguishable school bus. He flipped to another channel and saw about the same thing there. He turned it off.

"Where are you!" he demanded.

"I don't know," she sobbed.

He ran into the bedroom and snatched up the GPS receiver he had bought, hoping never to have to use it. He turned it on, and the scanner went around two times then beeped that it had found the target.

"What are you by?" he asked, in a reassuring voice.

"Some trees and a farm, by a red barn," she answered as she looked around again.

"Alright, I'll be there shortly," he promised as he ran to the garage and jumped into the Viper. Joanne would have to wait.

At 80 MPH, a lot of ground can be covered in a short amount of time. Ian tracked Maris down in the farmer's field. He had not even bothered to ask permission to be there. The guy would just have to figure it out for himself what the parachute was doing on his property.

When he found her she was a pathetic mess of tangled brown hair and tears. He handed her some bottled water and she eagerly drank it down. He carried her out to the road where the car was and fastened her in. He started the car and they headed for the hospital.

They showed up at the Emergency Room to a virtual mob scene of people. Angry parents were screaming, demanding to know the condition of their children or if they were even alive. Ian was about to leave and go to another hospital when a policeman walked up behind him and squeezed his shoulder with his meaty hand.

"Help ya sir?" the policeman demanded.

"Yes, my daughter is hurt," Ian answered as he winced in discomfort.

"Come with me," the policeman ordered.

Ian looked at Maris and shrugged. With this many people he could not understand why the policeman picked him. He led them down a hall and pushed open a door where he motioned them inside. The door closed behind them and two men in rumpled suits were sitting at a wooden table in what appeared to be their makeshift office.

"Mr. James," the guy on the left stood up and extended his hand to Ian. He still had Maris in his arms so he just nodded.

"I am Agent Burke and this is Agent Fry. We are with the FAA and your wife has been in a little bit of an accident," he explained calmly.

Ian nodded again and said nothing. Burke just stared at him.

"She's going to be alright," Fry stated.

Ian breathed a sigh of relief and Maris sniffled as she buried her face in Ian's shoulder.

"Seems your wife's plane hit a bus full of kids, and most of them weren't so lucky."

Ian nodded again and breathed deeply.

"Your wife drunk much?" Burke asked.

"OK, that's it. What is a freaking bus doing on a runway!" Ian demanded. "My daughter needs medical attention and we are playing '20 Questions'!" Ian growled.

"Don't get upset, Mr. James, it is procedure to ask questions. A nurse stepped into the room and took Maris from Ian so she could be examined.

"She is lucky to be alive, ya know?" Fry offered.

"Who?"

"Your wife, she took a pretty big fall out of the sky," Burke answered.

"She's tough," Ian stated.

"Alright Mr. James, that is all we have for you now."

"Can I see her?"

"She is in surgery, it will be a while. We will let you know," Burke answered.

Ian turned around, jerked the door open, and walked out.

Eugene Gregg shivered in the back of the squad car. They had driven past the City Jail to the County Detention Center. The car pulled inside the fenced-in area and the gate closed behind them. Tibbits and Palmer climbed out of the car and then jerked Eugene out of the back seat and led him to the detention center for check-in. A balding guard wearing glasses sat at a desk to fill out the paperwork. He took all the information off of Eugene's driver's license, then looked up at Tibbits and Palmer.

"And what's the charge Captain?" he asked, his pen hanging over the paperwork.

Palmer looked at Tibbits.

"Child endangerment," Palmer growled. Tibbits looked at the floor.

"That's bad," the guard sighed, as he finished writing on the forms. "You live to tell about that."

He stood up and led the trio to the common room where the prisoners slept. The guard opened the door and shoved Eugene into the dimly lit room. A couple of inmates sat up on their bunks.

"What's the charge?" one of them asked.

"Child endangerment," the guard answered as he slammed the heavy metal door closed. Several inmates sat up out of their beds. They all looked at Eugene.

The guard returned to his desk. He heard a call for help, a shout of anger, and a plea for mercy. The calls fell upon deaf ears.

CHAPTER 14

"How do you feel?" Ian whispered to Joanne as he leaned over her hospital bed. Her eyes closed, she shook her head slightly.

"Like a jigsaw puzzle with a couple of pieces gone?" he asked.

She nodded.

Maris limped over and wrapped her arms around her mom. "I love you," she whispered. Joanne nodded.

She laid there for a while and Ian put a straw to her mouth. She drank some water. She rolled over onto her back and her eyes came open for the first time in days. She looked up at Ian. "Where is my plane?" she croaked.

He shook his head and looked away. Tears welled up in her eyes and rolled down her cheeks. He leaned over to kiss the tears away and she turned her head. Ian sighed and sat down.

"They gave me a pink cast Mom," Maris announced. Joanne nodded.

"How much longer do I have to be here?" Joanne murmured.

"I don't know."

"What do you mean you don't know?" she growled as she turned to face them.

"Until they say you can go I guess," Ian offered. Joanne took a deep breath. "How long have I been here?" she wanted to know.

"A week," Ian answered. Joanne rolled over onto her side and found the nurse call button. She pressed it twice with her thumb. A moment later a nurse appeared at the door. "Get me a doctor," she demanded.

"Mrs. James. . ."

"Now!" Joanne snapped. The nurse turned on her heel and walked away. Ian looked at Maris. She had an odd look on her face. In the past, Ian had been able to keep Maris from seeing Joanne get ugly. But now he thought Maris might see Joanne in all her glory.

A black man in surgical scrubs arrived at the door.

"Doctor," Joanne cooed.

"Dr. Page," the man said as he held out his hand. Joanne managed to lift her hand off the bed to briefly shake hands.

"How am I doing doctor?"

"Good," he answered.

"Great, can I go?" she asked.

The doctor smiled. "You are doing good for someone who fell out of the sky Mrs. James."

Joanne's eyes narrowed.

"You will be stabilized in about a week, then you can leave the hospital. But you will have to be back here to do physical therapy."

Joanne looked away. That is not what she wanted to hear. The doctor talked about all the physical therapy she would need to do – she barely listened. Ian and Maris stood wide-eyed while listening to all she was going to have to do to recover.

A week later Ian rolled Joanne out of the hospital in a wheelchair and gingerly placed her into the Lincoln. He drove her home and carried her to the couch. She thanked him and went to sleep.

The next morning he prepared her breakfast and shared with her the therapy the doctor wanted her to work on. She looked at the paper and laid it on the coffee table. "Later," she whispered.

Later on he brought her lunch. After that she dozed off to sleep. She woke up and he brought her dinner. They watched some television, then he stroked her neck and her back until she fell asleep. Then he went to bed.

That went on for a week with Joanne doing a little therapy when she felt like doing it. They returned to the hospital for the doctor to evaluate her progress. There was little to report. The doctor recommended Ian take Joanne to a physical therapist. He provided the name of one who was covered by their insurance. After Ian talked to Joanne about the situation, she agreed to go.

Ian and Maris got up each day and took Joanne to therapy. Maris worked on her lessons there, as Joanne began the slow process of recovery.

At the end of the summer Ian decided he could not continue to home-school Maris and also help with therapy, so he enrolled her into public school. Maris was somewhat reluctant. She was concerned she would not be as scholarly as the other seventh-graders. Ian told her she would be fine. She would make friends, go to school dances, maybe be on a sports team. Maris was not so sure. She did not know what to think about riding the bus to school, especially after Joanne's accident, or changing classes each hour.

Ian took her shopping and bought her some new clothes. They went to a salon and she got a haircut. The first day he stood with her at the end of the driveway until the bus came, then he followed the bus to school, driving the Del Sol, as she thought it looked like a jelly bean on wheels.

When she got off the bus she waved and cautiously walked into the foreboding building for her first day of group education.

After a week it turned out that her dad was right – she fit right in with the other girls. When they talked about some of the places they wanted to go or things they wanted to do, she would smile and look down. She had already done many of those things.

One day a new girl showed up in her homeroom class. She was lanky with straight, long blonde hair. She had a ready smile and a soft voice.

"Hi, I am Maris," she said at lunch as the new girl looked for a place to sit. "Come with me." Maris led her around to one corner of the lunchroom where there were two empty spots.

"This is where I sit," she explained casually. "My dad taught me to sit at the corner of the room so you can see everything."

"What is he a gunfighter?" the new girl laughed.

"He's a winner," Maris stated firmly.

"Be cool, I was just kidding," the new girl apologized.

"When you are at a new school you have to make sure you are friends with the right people."

"How many times have you been in a new school?" Maris asked.

The new girl hesitated as she counted in her head. "Six," she answered.

"Why?" Maris gasped.

"My mom's work," the girl mumbled as she looked down at her lunch. She dug in and took a bite.

"Well maybe you will stay here for a while," Maris answered, seeing that the girl did not want to talk about her mom's work.

"I'm new here also," she offered.

"You are? It seems like it is no big deal."

"It's not."

"OK, I am Lacrisha."

"Nice to meet you, Lacrisha."

They shared another class in the afternoon and went their separate ways on the buses.

When Maris arrived home she was surprised to see the Lincoln in the driveway. Joanne's therapy should not be over for an hour yet. She walked in through the garage between the Daytona and the Viper. She could almost feel their power coursing through her body when she walked past them. She padded up the steps to the kitchen. The solid door was open and she looked through the screen door.

Joanne was lying on the couch and Ian was standing in front of the television. "I just don't care," Joanne stated. "They said I can't fly anymore, no matter what I do. I just want to die."

Ian shook his head. "No, you will not quit on our daughter like your mom quit on you. She needs you, I need you."

Joanne laughed derisively. "You needed me for a baby, and that's it. Look at this place, you do everything. You don't need me."

"I do it for you. I will let you do whatever you want," Ian stated.

"I don't want to do anything," Joanne sighed, "I'm dead."

"You're not!" Ian bristled.

Joanne rolled over, her head facing the cushion. She was done talking.

Ian looked down at his hand and contorted it into a claw. He focused his eyes on his palm for an answer – as always, there never was one. He walked into the kitchen to prepare dinner.

Maris backed down the steps and wiped tears from her eyes with her sleeve. She fanned her flushed face with her notebook so they would not know she had heard them. After a couple of minutes she climbed the steps and pulled the door open.

"Hi Babe," her dad greeted her with a smile and a hug.

Maris smiled back. "I made a new friend today," she announced.

"Oh, and what is her name?" Ian asked as he pulled a box from the cupboard.

"Her name is Lacrisha."

"Pardon," Ian coughed. "What did you say?"

"Lacrisha."

"Really, wow, that's an unusual name."

"Yes, she is new here. She came from California."

"Wow, that's a long way away from here," Ian observed.

"She said her mom has a job that she has had to move around a lot."

Ian cleared his throat. "Well OK, let's get ready for dinner."

CHAPTER 15

As it turned out, with Lacrisha having grown up in California, she had been to Mexico many times so she was fluent in Spanish. She and Maris became fast friends. When they did not want the other girls to know what they were talking about, which was about all the time, they spoke in Spanish. They spoke Spanish on the telephone to each other and sometimes text-messaged in Spanish.

"Can Lacrisha spend the weekend?" Maris asked Ian one night during dinner. Ian coughed and looked over at Maris.

"You think?"

"Yeah dad, she is really cool. She speaks Spanish. When we talk it seems like there is no one else in the room because nobody else knows what we are talking about."

Ian looked down at the uneaten food on his plate and took a breath. "Do you really think this is a good idea with your mom and her condition?"

Maris thought for a moment, then walked out into the front room where Joanne was propped up on the couch, instant-messaging a friend on her laptop computer.

"Mom," Maris whispered.

"Huh," Joanne mumbled as she briefly took her eyes off the screen to acknowledge her daughter before she was back to the keyboard.

"Is it alright if I have a girl from school come over and spend the weekend?" Maris asked.

"Uh huh," Joanne answered, not looking up this time.

"Thank you," she breathed as she leaned over and gave her mom an awkward hug.

She came back to the kitchen and sat down. "She said it was alright."

Ian looked down at his plate. "Alright, I'll talk to her parents," he sighed.

"You don't have to do that."

"What?" Ian asked, confused.

"She lives with her mom, her dad lives in a town called San Quentin," Maris explained.

"Great," Ian gulped.

Later that night Ian punched the number Maris had given him into the telephone. It rang, then it rang again. With each ring the tightness in his chest increased – he felt like he was calling for a date.

"Hello," a young voice answered breathlessly.

"Mrs. McClain please," Ian squeaked.

"May I ask who is calling?"

"Ian James," he gasped.

"Hold please," the young voice said. The handset went down and Ian motioned Maris to bring him a drink. She put a glass under the faucet and filled it halfway before giving it to Ian. He knocked it back like a shot glass. Maris' eyes bulged at the ease in which he had put the contents of the glass away.

"Hello," an older, breathy voice said into the receiver.

"Hi, this is Ian James," he said, his voice trembling.

"Long time no hear," the voice responded smoothly.

"Yes, it is nice to meet you, on the phone I mean," Ian coughed.

"Little ears?"

"Yes, a nice day. So, my daughter would like for your daughter to spend the weekend, watch a movie, eat popcorn. 'Girl stuff' I guess."

"You know a lot about spending time with girls don't you?" the voice responded.

Ian coughed two times. "So you say you will bring your daughter over at six o'clock Friday for dinner then?"

The voice laughed a familiar laugh. "That will be fine, see you then. I have missed you." The phone clicked on the other end.

"OK, we will see you then," Ian chuckled.

He turned and faced Maris.

"Nice lady," he laughed. She did a celebratory fist-pump.

Friday evening at 5:59 a black SUV nosed into the lane leading from the road to the farmhouse. It came to a stop at the top of the hill on the plateau outside the garage. A lanky blonde woman wearing mirror sunglasses climbed out of the driver's side and pulled an overnight bag out of the back seat. The passenger door opened and a younger, lanky blonde with her hair pulled back in a ponytail emerged.

Inside the garage the screen door slammed and Maris raced out, her shoulder-length brown hair waving in the breeze. She wrapped her arms around Lacrisha and gave her a welcome hug as they shared a laugh. Rachelle McClain handed her daughter the overnight bag and with a smirk on her face waved at Ian as he stood at the garage door. He smiled and waved back.

"This is Lacrisha," Maris gushed, her round face beaming with pride as she savored each letter of the name.

"Nice to meet you," Ian responded, as he shook the young girl's hand and looked into her piercing Kelly-green eyes. He glanced up as the SUV drove away.

"Thank you, Mr. James," Lacrisha answered softly, her full lips breaking into a pleasant smile under her small nose. Ian carried her bag inside. Maris introduced Lacrisha to Joanne after they entered the house and she nodded acknowledgement from the couch.

The delivery pizza arrived minutes later and the two girls devoured a couple of pieces, drank some soda, then headed to Maris' bedroom.

"Tonight, a classic," she proclaimed as she held the VHS tape above her head.

"Are you sure?" Lacrisha asked, wrinkling her nose.

"Oh yes, it has a cool car," Maris explained as she slipped the movie "Starman" into the machine. The credits rolled and Maris pulled out her photo album from a shelf. She flipped the book open and showed

Lacrisha pictures of her growing up, going to car shows, and her trip to Japan.

"That's cool," Lacrisha observed, pointing to a picture of Maris in a red kimono at Barbra's sister's house outside Tokyo.

"Maybe Mom can take us to a resort in Mexico," Lacrisha offered. They agreed that sounded like fun. They kept flipping pages and watching the movie until Lacrisha stopped on one page. There was what appeared to be a picture cut in half.

"Who is that?" Lacrisha asked.

Maris studied it for a moment, then pointed out the door. "That is my dad at a car show," she explained.

"He looks like a kid."

"He used to be a kid," Maris stated.

Lacrisha bit her lip. "It seems like I have seen that picture somewhere before."

Maris looked at it again. It was of Ian at the first May Day Car Show – he was standing by the front wheel of a black car with silver stripes on the side. His head was slightly turned towards the back of the car. He appeared to be looking at someone. Apparently the picture had been cut in half and the person in the other half had the rest of it.

She shrugged and pulled the picture out of the book and turned it over. Written on the back were the words "Third Place" in handwriting she did not recognize. Lacrisha had gotten up to go to the bathroom, so Maris slipped the picture back in the book.

Lacrisha returned with a panicked look on her face. "I forgot my retainer," she moaned. "I cannot sleep without it."

"Let's go tell my dad," Maris suggested as she stood up. The girls walked back into the kitchen.

"Ready for some popcorn?" Ian asked.

"She forgot her retainer," Maris explained.

"Oh. Alright Rachelle. Let's call your mom and I will go get it for you," Ian said.

"Pardon?" Lacrisha asked.

"I'll go get it," Ian repeated cheerfully.

"You called me by my mom's name," Lacrisha stated.

"Oh, I am sorry about that. She told me her name last night on the phone. Right, your name is Lacrisha and your mom's name is Rachelle."

Lacrisha seemed to accept the explanation and called her house to let Rachelle know that Ian would be there.

"OK, I'll be back," Ian called from the door, directions in hand. He backed the Del Sol out of the driveway and made his way through town to the new housing addition. He found the correct cul-de-sac and pulled into the driveway. When he got out of the car his knees buckled and he steadied himself on the fender. He took a couple of deep breaths and knocked on the front door. The door was pulled open and Rachelle was standing on the other side of the screen. "Long time no see," she stated smoothly.

Ian nodded and cleared his throat.

She unlatched the screen door and eased it open. Ian stepped in and saw that there were still boxes to be unpacked, and a few pictures were on the walls. "Still getting settled in," Rachelle explained.

She reached down and picked the retainer case off the end table. "Is this what you want?" she whispered. They made eye contact, and Ian lowered his head and stepped forward to accept the plastic case from her hand. His wrist rubbed against her arm during the exchange and she exhaled. They stood there, wrist to wrist, then slowly Ian looked up into her face and saw her shiny green eyes. He reached out and gave her a hug. She hugged him back. They stood there in each other's arms as the minutes passed.

"Am I holding on too long?" she croaked.

Ian took a deep breath, reached down, and picked her up. He carried her over to the couch and gently kissed her face – she turned her head a little each time so he would connect where she wanted him to kiss. Along her forehead, down by her ear, cheek, and chin. Then she turned and he landed on her lips and she kissed him back.

"Stop it," he growled. "You don't have to do that for me."

"It's been so long," she whimpered.

He breathed and kissed her on the lips. She opened her mouth.

"What am I doing?" she asked herself aloud.

"That sounds like a Harlequin," he mumbled as he pulled away.

"Why did you come back?" he asked as he stood up over her.

"Why didn't you go with me?" she responded.

"I couldn't, I was a big fish in a small pond. That baseball scholarship was my only chance to go to college."

"Out there you would have been a big fish in a big pond," she stated.

"Come on Rachelle, how would that have been? You were 16 years old and I was 18. You made six movies in ten years. Plus, you were in a television show. Where would I have fit into that?"

"I had a 2300-square-foot home, you would have fit fine."

"Then why did you go?" he wanted to know.

"I couldn't stay here," she sighed. She opened up one of the boxes and pulled out a photo album. She flipped through a few pages until she found what she was looking for. She pointed to a picture that looked like it had been cut in half. She was standing by a black car with a silver stripe on the side, holding a Third Place trophy in her hands.

"My agent saw me in this picture and he liked it. He thought I could go places, do things. Because of you I got to get out of here."

Ian lowered his head – he felt like he had gotten kicked in the gut. He wanted to throw up, he hacked and dry-heaved. Rachelle led him to the bathroom where he fell to his knees and gagged, leaning over the toilet. She stroked his back and clasped his hand. Eventually he rolled over. She ran some water over a washcloth and rang it out in the sink. She ran the cool material over his face. He rolled her beneath him into his arms.

"You smell good," he whispered as he kissed her on the face. A tear fell from his eye and rolled down her cheek. She looked up at him and he could see that her eyes were watery.

"I'm sorry," she whispered.

"You don't have to apologize to me," he stated. He kissed her cheek, then staggered to his feet. She stood up and they were still holding hands. He could not let her go, she did not want to let go.

Finally he reached over with his other hand and pried their fingers apart. They looked into each other's eyes. He turned and strode to the front door where he had lost the plastic case on the carpet. He picked it up and walked out to the Del Sol. He climbed into the car and wiped his face with his sleeve.

By the time he arrived back home, his face was no longer flushed. He handed Lacrisha the plastic case and went to his bedroom to take a shower. She watched him as he walked away. She thought she could smell her mom's perfume. She concluded it must have come from when her mom touched the plastic case.

Chapter 16

Sitting at the kitchen table Sunday afternoon Ian worked through the bills until the checkbook was nearly dry. He sighed as he stood up. Stepping over to the screen door he looked out into the garage as he took a sip of ice water. At the far end of the garage was the white and orange Dodge Charger Daytona residing under a cotton car cover. Next to that and facing out was his Dodge Viper. Next was his convertible Lincoln. Closest to the door was Joanne's Dodge Charger SRT-8. The Del Sol sat outside in its own spot at the edge of the driveway where sometimes Ian would let Maris drive it around on the flat part of the yard.

He took another sip of water and strolled across the kitchen. He could hear Maris and Lacrisha in the bedroom as he stepped into the front room where Joanne was propped up on the couch with a smile on her face as she instant-messaged someone.

Ian cleared his throat as he sat down and looked at her. Joanne looked up blank-faced at Ian, as if to ask what he wanted.

"I was doing the bills," Ian stated.

Joanne just looked at him. "With your disability payments and me working part-time we are just barely making it," he explained.

Joanne glanced at her computer, then back at Ian. "There is a classic car auto auction coming up. . ."

"I am NOT selling the Daytona," Joanne stated icily.

Ian exhaled and nodded. "I am thinking I am going to put the Viper up," he offered. Joanne relaxed and looked back at the screen. "It's your car," she said.

Silence.

"Yeah, remember how we first met, I was driving it," Ian recalled fondly. Joanne looked up and her eyes softened momentarily, then she turned serious again. "Yeah, that was a while ago," she breathed.

He smiled at her and she looked back at the screen. "You want to go?" he asked hopefully.

"Where?"

"To the auction."

"How long is it?"

"Most of the day."

Joanne rolled her eyes. "I couldn't do that," she stated flatly.

Ian nodded. "Yeah," he agreed. He lifted himself up out of the chair and headed back toward the kitchen. Halfway there he heard the girls again in the bedroom and sauntered down the hall. They were speaking in Spanish so he knocked on the door, which was ajar.

The Spanish stopped.

"Yes?" Maris asked.

Ian eased the door open to find the girls sitting on the floor, pouring over Mexico resort brochures they had picked up at the mall when he had taken them shopping.

"Planning a trip?" he asked casually.

"Is it OK?" Maris asked, with pleading eyes.

"We'll see," Ian answered.

The girls cheered, because that usually meant "yes".

"Want to go to an auto auction with me?" he interjected.

Both girls looked up wide-eyed.

"I'm gonna let the Viper go," he explained.

Maris gasped as she leaped up and wrapped her arms around his waist. "It's your car Daddy," she whimpered.

"Oh Baby, it was never my car. I was just taking care of it until the next person has it," he explained.

She relaxed her grip, stood back and looked up at him. "Really?" she asked.

"Yeah, really."

She considered this for a moment then sat down. She looked over at Lacrisha, who had said nothing. "Can she go too?"

"If it is alright with her mom."

Lacrisha looked up and smiled. "Cool beans."

That night when Ian and Maris took Lacrisha home, they talked to Rachelle in the somewhat less-cluttered front room.

"If Joanne isn't going, perhaps I should," Rachelle offered casually. "If the girls need to go to the bathroom and all."

The girls looked to Ian, and he pretended to contemplate the idea then shrugged as if he had been defeated. "Three to one, how could I not say yes?" he asked, as he threw up his hands in mock defeat.

As Ian and Maris stepped to the door to leave, Ian looked back and caught Rachelle's eye. He winked at her and she smiled.

CHAPTER 17

Two weeks later Ian and Maris drove the Viper down to the arena where the event was to occur, with Rachelle and Lacrisha following in the black SUV. Red carpets were laid out on the floor in front of the auctioneer stand and flat-screen televisions were placed throughout the 400-chair seating area for bidders to keep track of the prices.

Ian checked in the Viper and took a final look at the car, then patted it on the fender. "Goodbye old friend," he whispered. Maris gave him a hug and they all four went upstairs to the restaurant for breakfast. It was mostly a somber mood and little was said.

After the meal they descended the stairs and stood for a while as one-by-one, the cars were pushed by hand to the front, details were announced, and then the bidding began. Some cars did not sell, as the reserve price was not reached. Occasionally the auctioneer would chastise the bidders for not bidding higher. Ian thought that was a terrible way to do business.

After several cars, the girls asked if they could go explore the collection of vehicles that numbered in the hundreds. Ian and Rachelle looked at each other and then the girls. "You got your GPS tracker?" Ian sternly asked Maris.

She nodded, tapping the seam of her jacket that it had been sown into. "Be careful and come back shortly," Ian stated. The girls nodded, clasped hands and disappeared into the sea of humanity and vintage metal.

Ian and Rachelle found two chairs together on the end of a row and sat down in front of one of the television stands. Rachelle laid her hand on the television stand and looked at Ian, and he shrugged. She pulled a promotional catalog out of the complimentary bag they had received and laid it over her hand, then looked at Ian again.

He looked around and casually reached his hand under the catalog and they interlocked fingers. Ian coughed and cleared his throat. Her warm hand felt good. A guy walked by selling bottled water. Ian waved him down and paid him. He handed the bottle to Rachelle who unscrewed the cap and took a drink. She passed it back to Ian, who held it to his mouth and swallowed.

"Dad!" Maris gasped, as she ran up from behind them. Lacrisha followed close behind. Ian turned around to see his ashen-faced daughter and immediately stood up to survey the crowd to see if somebody was running away. "Your car is here," she announced breathlessly.

"Of course it is, we drove it here," Ian stated.

"No, the black one," Maris explained.

Rachelle stood bolt upright to look at the girls' blank faces, then she scanned down the auction list page. She did not see the car, then she turned it over and discovered that there were more on the back. Ian leaned over to take a look and their eyes fell upon the listing at the same time. They both gasped as they read: "1973 Mercury Montego GT 428, 4-speed, black and silver inside and out". It was #225, to be auctioned at about 1:30. Ian coughed.

"Where?" he demanded.

Maris took his hand and led him down an aisle past some vintage pickup trucks and a pace car, and then in the middle of the row sat the black and silver car. It looked the same as the car in the picture from long ago, wheels and everything. Squared off in the front and rounded in the back, it looked like it would be more aerodynamic going backwards. The motor made all the difference.

Ian breathed in through his teeth and looked over at Rachelle, who was wide-eyed, seeing the ghost car from her past. Random memories of time spent with Ian in the car tumbled through her mind.

"Wow," he finally uttered, "That sure is something." Rachelle nodded – she was strangely speechless. They looked the car over some more and picked up a card that contained all the details from the passenger seat. Ian opened the driver's door, climbed in and started up the car as the key was attached to the steering column with a plastic tie. The engine cranked and rumbled smoothly to life. He tapped the gas and the rumble increased, a beautiful sound to hear again.

He looked up at Rachelle standing at the door, her hand over her mouth. Ian cut off the engine and climbed out of the car, pressing the door closed as he did. "Well, the Viper is set to go at 1:00 so we ought to be around to see this go," he offered, with a weak smile.

All three of the women looked solemnly back at him. Silently they all walked back to where they had been seated. The chairs had filled up. They climbed the stairs and returned to the restaurant where they ate French fries and drank soda.

At 12:50 they returned to the floor. The Viper was behind a '60's Mustang and a '70's Chevelle. The cars were pushed in front of the people and bid upon. The Mustang did not meet the reserve price and was rolled away, and the Chevelle was sold.

"Here we have a bone-stock first-generation Dodge Viper, red with tan interior. No reserve, so this will be the next car to sell," the auctioneer announced. He began the bidding.

Ian glanced down at Maris. She had her head buried in his arm. "It's alright," he whispered. She buried her head deeper.

"Did Joanne ever drive it?" Rachelle asked.

Ian cocked his head, looked at her sideways and raised his eyebrow.

"Did she?" Rachelle asked again.

Ian nodded slowly.

"Can she drive?"

"She thinks she can," Ian whispered with a smirk.

"Not so much?"

Ian shook his head. "She was hard on it, like everything she gets, she eventually breaks it," Ian explained.

She saw hurt in his eyes. "Like your heart?" she whispered.

Ian nodded slowly.

"Do you think she ever loved you?" she continued in a hushed voice.

Ian smiled. "She had a crush on me."

"How about her?" Rachelle asked, pointing at Maris' buried head. "Is she breaking her?"

Ian nodded, and this time he wasn't smiling. "You see how she clings to Lacrisha. They are more inseparable than sisters, close, like David and Jonathan in the Bible."

The bidding slowed and the auctioneer pushed to get the final bid. "$27,000 once, twice, sold." Ian smiled.

Maris pulled away. "Now we can get our car," she stated as she wiped a tear from her face.

Ian coughed and raised his eyebrows. "We'll see."

They walked out of the hall and the girls sat at a table while Ian went to Registration to get the check for the sale of the car. He folded it up and put it in his wallet as he walked back to the table. They sat there and drank lemonade until 1:25. Refreshed and ready, they strode back out onto the floor. A souped-up station wagon with a blower sticking out of the hood was not getting enough bids to meet the reserve, so it was passed for an ancient Jeep which also had too high of a reserve to sell.

Then the big black and silver Mercury was rolled into place as the auctioneer announced, "1973 Mercury Montego GT 428, 4-speed, 77,000 miles, an older restoration." He started at $10,000 and nobody bid so he dropped to $7,000, $5,000, then $3,000. Somebody's hand went up and the auction began.

Ian had his hand hanging at his side. Rachelle wrapped her pinkie-finger and thumb around his pointer-finger and started slowly stroking his finger. Ian's other hand immediately went up to place a bid.

A white-haired man on the other side of the room was involved. Rachelle looked over and saw he had a young trophy wife. Rachelle handed the bottled water to the girls and pointed her finger menacingly at the woman for the girls to see.

They looked over at the woman and nodded. She stroked Ian's finger and his shot up. The girls walked over by the woman who was wearing a white blouse and light green slacks.

"Atrocious," Maris and Lacrisha said in unison.

The bidding slowed until it was just Ian and the white-haired man. Lacrisha unscrewed the bottle cap and Ian placed a bid. A screech went up as the cold water splashed on the woman's green slacks and the white-haired man looked over at his trophy wife.

"Sold," the auctioneer said. Ian had won. Lacrisha and Maris slipped away as people dabbed napkins on the floor to sop up the water.

Ian walked back to Registration to hand in the check he had received – he had a different one when he returned. The girls mobbed him with hugs, and Rachelle slipped a kiss on his far-side cheek that the girls could not see.

They returned to the restaurant upstairs to celebrate with ice cream. After they were done they walked downstairs to where the cars were lined up and received the keys. Ian and Maris climbed into the front seat and he started the engine. "Beautiful," he said again as he looked out the window at Rachelle, who was standing by the door. She smiled back at him.

The black car with a silver stripe on the side climbed the driveway and came to a stop in front of the garage doors. Ian and Maris went inside. Joanne had dozed off on the couch. Ian had Maris get into bed after a late dinner. He went back outside to the black Mercury. He felt like he was 18 years old again as he looked at the car. He climbed inside, drove down the lane to the road, and headed for the gas station. He pulled in between the pumps and went inside to prepay. He dropped the money on the counter and nodded to the cashier. The cashier nodded and waved as Ian headed out the door to pump the gas.

The gauge read nearly full as he drove down the road to the new housing addition. When he pulled into the cul-de-sac there was still a light on in the house. He climbed the porch steps and knocked softly on the metal storm door. He heard some movement inside and the door came open. Rachelle stood there, hands on hips, wondering if she should invite him in or not.

"What are you doing?" she screeched lightly.

"Going for a ride, wanna go?"

"Are you crazy?"

"Yes."

"Alright then." She walked back to her bedroom and reappeared shortly wearing her sneakers, and stepped out onto the porch. Ian took her hand, led her to the passenger side of the car, and opened the door for her. He went around to the other side, climbed in and started the car. The mighty engine rumbled to life. They drove out of the neighborhood, back to the road, away from the housing addition.

They rode in silence, each flashing back to a time years ago when they were younger. Ian took his hand off the gearshift and rested it upon her hand atop the console between the seats. He slowed at a thin road that cut through the trees and crept along the winding path to a shelter house. He pulled into the parking lot and shut off the car. They sat there looking straight ahead out the windshield at the dark woods.

"This is where your class party was," she whispered.

Ian nodded. "This is where you said goodbye."

She nodded and lowered her head. Tears came to her eyes and fell into her lap. "I never meant to hurt you," she sobbed softly.

"I know," he whispered.

She leaned over and gently kissed him on the cheek, then on his chin. She opened her door and climbed into the back seat, laying her head on the armrest. He climbed out and got into the back with her. With his left knee in the floor pan and his right knee up in the seat he straddled her, looking into her eyes. She smiled and pulled up her shirt just enough so that he could see that she had written "Vacancy" across her tummy with lipstick. He smiled and bent down as she closed her eyes. He gently kissed her neck and her breathing slowed.

He straightened up and she looked at him. He had an odd look on his face, as if he was confused, and did not know what to do next.

"Why did you do all this?" she breathed.

"I just wanted it to feel like it used to," he explained.

"Does it?" she asked as she cleared her dry throat.

"Yes and no," he answered. "Yes it feels the same, but no, I know I have to go home and that sickens me."

She closed her eyes. "Me too."

He opened the door and climbed out. He opened her door so she could get out. They got back into the front of the car and he took her home. He returned to the farmhouse, took a shower, and went to bed.

Chapter 18

"So how come ya got another car?" Joanne asked, looking up from the computer as Ian brought her breakfast.

"I had one like it before," Ian answered, surprised that Joanne would even notice or care.

"What did Lacrisha's mother think of it?" Joanne continued.

Ian stopped and looked at Joanne. "Why?"

"I just wondered."

"Why?" Ian asked again.

"So, how did she like it?"

"She liked it fine."

"Is there anything else?"

"What?" Ian snorted.

"Did you take her for a ride?"

Ian nodded.

"Why?" she asked.

Ian raised his hands from his sides and held them out, palms up. "What is the deal?"

"Where did you take her?"

Ian exhaled. "To the shelter house."

"Why?"

"That is where she said goodbye to me when she moved to L. A."

"So she was your girlfriend?"

"OK, yes, she was my girlfriend."

"Do you still love her?"

"No," Ian snapped.

"Does she still love you?"

Ian looked away and walked back into the kitchen. Joanne put the breakfast tray down on the end table and followed him into the kitchen.

"So she still loves you after all this time. Does she want to have your baby?"

Ian spun around. "Don't say that again," he growled.

Maris walked into the kitchen and her mouth dropped open when she heard Ian raise his voice. She had never seen him get upset like that before. Joanne saw Maris and retreated to the front room to eat. Maris looked at her dad with eyes of wonder.

"Are you getting a divorce?" she asked with a quivering voice.

"No," Ian grunted.

Maris exhaled. She picked up her sack lunch that Ian had made for her and gave him a hug, then she headed down to the bus stop. Ian looked through the cupboards to see what lunch would be. When Joanne was done eating she brought the empty tray into the kitchen and returned to instant-messaging on the couch.

Saturday morning the nose of the black Mercury pulled out of the lane and headed down the highway to Camille's greasy spoon restaurant.

"This is where your mom and I met and shared our first meal," Ian offered, like it was the first time he had told Maris the story. She nodded dutifully. They ordered and she talked about school and about a guy by the name of Wes, who had asked her to the dance. Ian nodded as he listened.

The food came. When they were done eating, Ian paid. They walked outside to the car and drove down the highway. Ian turned on the radio and Maris sang along, as she knew the song on the classic radio station. A black SUV pulled out of the new housing addition. "There is Lacrisha and her mom," Maris squealed.

They followed the black SUV through two lights, then the SUV turned into the Wal-Mart parking lot. "They are going where we are going!" Maris gasped. The black SUV pulled into a parking place. Rachelle and Lacrisha climbed out.

Maris unbuckled her seatbelt, got out of the car and raced over to Lacrisha to give her a hug. The three of them waited until Ian arrived and then they continued to walk toward the store. Rachelle, wearing her mirror sunglasses, nodded at Ian.

"Good song," she whispered.

"Thank you," Ian nodded back. He excused himself as he had to pick up some things and would catch up with them later. He headed to the checkout stand and picked up a handful of postcards, then went to the back to pick up some motor oil.

They met up later, cashed out, and went their separate ways home.

Later that day Ian was in the garage writing when Maris walked up behind him. "What ya doin'?" she asked.

"Writing a postcard to Grandma," he stammered.

"In the garage?" she asked.

"Uh, yeah. Just a note." He slipped it into the console of the Mercury. "I'll mail it on the way to work."

Maris nodded.

The next Saturday Ian took Maris to her soccer game. Lacrisha was waiting when they pulled in. She waved and Maris waved back. Ian turned off the radio and strolled out to the sidelines, where Rachelle was on a chaise lounge.

"Good one," she breathed.

Ian nodded. After the game the girls waved goodbye before they climbed into their vehicles and drove to their homes.

One day after driving the Del Sol around in the yard, Maris walked through the garage past the Mercury. She wondered if Ian had remembered to mail the postcard that he had slipped into the console. She pulled open the car door and flipped open the console. She was surprised to find several postcards. She picked up the top one, which was addressed to the classic radio station that they listened to. In the "Comments" section was a request to play a song, with the time to play it. Maris furrowed her brow and placed it back in the console, gently snapping the lid closed.

She climbed the steps and walked into the kitchen. She walked over to the refrigerator to get a drink and her eyes fell on her soccer schedule. She looked at the time of the game and realized it was thirty minutes after the song was to be played. She wondered.

Ian walked into the kitchen carrying Joanne's empty tray. "Can I spend the night with Lacrisha?" she asked.

Ian shrugged. "Ask your mom and ask Lacrisha's mom," Ian answered.

Maris strode into the front room and asked Joanne, who grunted and nodded. Maris went to her bedroom and called Lacrisha. Lacrisha asked Rachelle, and it was set.

Friday Ian drove Maris over to the house, waved as she walked inside, and backed the car out of the driveway. The girls stayed up half the night. The next morning they put on their soccer uniforms, climbed into the black SUV and headed toward the soccer fields. Rachelle flicked on the radio and a tune from the classic radio station whiffed through the cabin. A couple more songs played. They were almost to the soccer fields when the song on the postcard came on. Maris saw that Rachelle was tapping out the beat on the steering wheel.

"Do you like that one?" Maris asked casually.

"It is a good one, it reminds me of when I was younger," Rachelle answered.

Maris slowly lowered her head. Her dad was sending songs to her best friend's mom.

When they reached the soccer fields Maris made a bee-line to the bathroom and vomited her breakfast. She did not feel any better. She told the coach she was sick and sat out the game. She sat silently in the car as Ian drove them home.

When the black car was in the garage she climbed out, walked up the steps and to her bedroom, where she closed her door and cried into her pillow.

CHAPTER 19

For her thirteenth birthday Maris wanted to visit the gravesite of her namesake, Roger Maris, in Fargo, North Dakota. In a rare show of cooperation, Joanne agreed to join Ian and Maris for the pilgrimage.

Ian visited the school to request Maris' assignments, as they were going to make a week of the trip and visit Mount Rushmore in South Dakota. The decision was made to take the Montego.

The big black Mercury crept down the lane to the highway and drove up to Camille's for breakfast. Then they pulled in next door to the gas station for a fill-up, then they were out onto the Interstate headed North. An hour into the trip they passed a sign that announced a car show.

"Can we go?" Maris asked hopefully.

"To the car show?" Ian queried, glancing up at the rear-view mirror into the pleading eyes of his daughter.

From the back seat Maris nodded. Ian glanced over at Joanne, who had her laptop computer open on her lap, pecking away at the keys. "Shall we go to a car show for our daughter's birthday? Like old times?"

Joanne raised her head up from the keyboard and looked directly at Ian. She had the same round brown eyes, the same ones he had first looked into years ago, but they were different now, more serious, almost without feelings.

"Whatever," she answered with a shrug of her shoulders, then she was back to typing on the keyboard.

Ian looked up into the rear-view mirror again and smiled at his daughter. "We're going to a car show," he announced. Maris exhaled and smiled back at her dad. She really enjoyed all the cars -- they were her old friends.

Ian came up behind a tractor-trailer that was lumbering along. He glanced into the side mirror and into the rear-view mirror. There were no cars, so he pulled out to pass the trailer and discovered that there was a line of cars in front of the truck. Ian down-shifted, the tires chirped and the Mercury hunkered down. He punched the accelerator and Earth's atmosphere was inhaled into the Ram-Air scoop sitting atop the hood. He passed the tractor and a station wagon. The tachometer was into the "yellow" when he speed-shifted seamlessly into third gear. Glued to the back seat, Maris watched breathlessly as the speedometer climbed.

The Mercury blew underneath the highway sign, informing them that the turn-off for the city where the car show was being held was at the top of the slight incline they were climbing.

With five cars to pass and a half-mile to go, Ian pulled the gearshift into fourth. "Let's see what ya got," Ian whispered as a smirk appeared on his face.

By then Joanne had looked up and realized they were quickly running out of road. Her fingers tapped the keyboard and she looked over at Ian and smiled. A voice came from the laptop.

"Do you want me to talk?" the voice asked.

"No Mr. Bond, I want you to die," another voice answered.

There was silence in the cabin of the car as all ears were tuned to the mighty motor as it strained to get every last bit of horsepower out of its cylinders. At 125 MPH they were going twice as fast as the vehicles they were trying to pass. In an agonizingly slow manner the final two cars fell behind them. Ian cranked the steering wheel and they flashed back into the right-hand lane. He let off the gas and pointed the car toward the circular exit ramp.

At three times the posted speed they raced into the exit. The rear wheels broke loose from the pavement and the car began to slide sideways down the ramp. Ian steered into the skid. Sparks flew from the rear bumper as it scraped along the concrete median that outlined the sweeping turn.

Ian glanced up and saw that the light at the bottom of the hill was red. There were no cars at the bottom of the hill, so the light had just turned. By then he had gotten the car down to 60 MPH, still too fast to stop. He saw daylight in the turn lane off to the right. Traffic or not, he could not yield. He shot past the "Yield" sign and cut in front of a woman driving a white van full of children. She immediately flipped him her middle finger. Joanne cranked down her window, held out both hands and returned the gesture, as Maris looked on wide-eyed. Ian cleared his throat and shook his head. He had regained control of the car and followed the car show signs that led them to the Town Square.

It was typical of most small town squares, with an historical courthouse in the center and a statue of a local patriot out front. Wrapped around the square were historic buildings, quaint shops, a soda fountain, hair salon, coffee shop, restaurant and a computer store. The show director pointed out a parking place at the far end and Ian crept past the other shiny cars and backed into the designated spot. They all climbed out and walked up to the check-in table. From there they found a hardware store and Ian purchased Joanne a chaise lounge chair and some suntan lotion. He paid a kid that worked there to carry the chair back to the car for Joanne, and she eagerly followed him. Ian went with Maris to look at the cars. They included the usual Chevelle's, Camero's, hot rods, Corvette's, Mustang's, and a couple of MOPAR's.

They looked at the cars for a while then stopped in for a drink. When they came out, Maris noticed in the front window of the computer store there was a plastic case for sale, just like the case for Joanne's computer. She pointed it out to Ian. He agreed it looked just like Joanne's case, and bought it as a back-up. The salesperson placed it in a sack and they worked their way back around to where the Mercury was parked. Joanne was stretched out on the lawn chair under a tree, typing away on the computer. Ian walked up and put the bag with the purchase in the trunk, unnoticed.

Ian and Maris were still standing beside the car when a burly man pushed past, almost knocking Maris down. She grabbed the bumper to steady herself and offered a weak "Excuse me," to the man, as he grunted at her.

In his thick arms he carried a small boy with yellowish skin, dark hair, and small dark eyes. In the boy's hands was a pair of Mickey Mouse sunglasses. As the man pushed through the wooden street barricade that was set up for the car show, the boy lost his grip on the glasses and they clattered to the ground. "Sir, you dropped these," Maris called out as she stepped forward to pick up the glasses. She looked into the little boy's eyes and wondered why the man did not have the boy facing forward as he carried him.

The man and the boy arrived at a white Oldsmobile parked across the street. The man pushed the boy into the back seat and climbed into the driver's seat, starting the car as he closed the door. Maris shrugged and turned back toward the car show with the glasses still in her hand. She heard some voices, almost frantic in their tone. What were they saying? It sounded familiar.

She looked down at the pavement to focus. She listened and her eyes opened wide. Her heart tightened up and her stomach rolled over. Then a man and a woman burst through the crowd, pushing an empty baby stroller.

"Where's my SON!" the man screamed in Japanese.

Maris looked up at Ian. "That man that just pushed by here kidnapped their son," she stated.

"What did he get into!" Ian snapped.

"A white Olds."

Ian raced around to the driver's side and jumped into the black Mercury, starting the car before the door was closed. The tires laid black lines as the Mercury knocked over the street barricade and roared down the street.

Maris walked up to the distraught couple and handed them the glasses. They screamed in agony as she explained to them in Japanese what had happened. A police officer arrived, as talk of the distraught couple spread. Maris explained to the officer what she had seen and that Ian had taken off after the Olds. The officer barked into his walkie-talkie and two wailing sirens pierced the air as two squad cars disappeared down the street.

Chapter 20

Ian caught sight of the white Olds two blocks from the square. It turned right to cut through a neighborhood headed back toward the Interstate. Ian ripped through the front yard of the house on the corner where the Olds had turned. He heard branches from the bushes in front of the house rake down the passenger side of the car. There was a gully at the far end of the yard. When the Mercury came out of the dip, the pavement ripped the front air dam just below the bumper, off of the car. The front and rear tires bent it into an unrecognizable shape.

The Mercury went airborne, then crashed to the street. Ian downshifted and burned the moisture from the back tires that they had picked up going through the yard. With a sudden burst of speed, he came up next to the Olds, cranked the steering wheel and slammed the passenger side into the driver's side of the Olds. The driver recovered and stayed on the road.

Ian jerked the wheel hard again and bashed the Olds. This time the driver over-corrected, lost control, and ran off the road. The Olds ran head-long into a tree, pushing the front bumper back and buckling both front fenders. The driver reached to push open the passenger door and it would not open. He tried his door, and it too was pinned closed by the buckled front fenders.

Ian got out and walked over to the Olds. He raised the window breaker device in his hand and shattered the window. The driver sat there wide-eyed before Ian punched him in the nose. Ian grabbed him by the back of the neck and slammed his face into the metal steering wheel. A torrent of blood poured from the unconscious man's nose.

Ian saw some movement in the back seat and reached his hand inside. A little cold hand squeezed his hand and Ian lifted the dazed little boy out.

Within seconds the two whining squad cars were on the scene. A third one raced up, and the horrified parents ran over to Ian to retrieve their child, sobbing uncontrollably as they did. A tow truck showed up and ripped the door off of the Olds, and the beefy policemen manhandled the driver into the squad car for what Ian surmised would be a memorable evening for everyone involved.

One of the policemen approached Ian to get his statement. He explained how Maris had concluded what had happened, and that he was just trying to help.

By then, neighbors were standing in their yards watching what was going on and a van with the local news showed up. Ian asked the driver of the tow truck if he could call in a flatbed truck for the Mercury. The reporter approached Ian so he obliged and repeated what he had told the policeman. When he was done the flatbed arrived and a second reporter approached, but Ian waved him off as the battered Mercury was hauled up onto the truck.

At the car show another group of reporters were gathered around Maris, drilling her with question after question. After almost an hour of explaining why she knew Japanese, she began to tire. Joanne finally stepped in to give Maris a break when another reporter approached. Joanne was about to cut the woman off when she recognized her as a reporter from the national news.

Exhausted, Maris sat down in the lawn chair and drowsily looked on as Joanne explained that it was her idea all along that her daughter be multi-cultural.

Maris shook her head wearily as hot tears boiled out of her brown eyes and trickled down her face. She stood up off the lawn chair and walked over to the policeman she had given her report to earlier.

"Could you take me to my daddy?" she pleaded, her eyes red and puffy. He looked down at the sad little girl and put in a call on the radio to find out where Ian and the car were. A call came back and they were informed that they were at a local body shop. The officer cut into Joanne's interview long enough to tell her he was taking Maris to the body shop, and then they were gone.

Maris walked into the noisy body shop. The Mercury was up on jacks. The front passenger fender, wheel and door had been removed. The rest of the side of the car had been sanded down to bare metal. The exhaust pipes hung loose from the bottom of the car, and a pair of legs wearing coveralls was sticking out from under the car. Maris tapped one of the legs with her foot and the person rolled out from under the car wearing a welding helmet and holding a blowtorch.

"Can you tell me where my Dad is?" Maris whimpered.

The person lifted up the helmet and Maris saw that it was Ian. She fell on his chest and sobbed. Ian patted her back as her tears streamed onto his face and rolled onto the coveralls. She dry-heaved. "Please don't make me go back," she pleaded.

"I can't make you do anything, Baby," he whispered.

"Let me stay here," she whined. "You always say to stay with the car during repairs."

Ian looked into his daughter's brown eyes and sighed. He nodded and they stood up as he took her hand. "Ya got a couch in the office?" he called to the guy in the paint booth. The guy nodded and pointed.

Ian followed the man's directions to a small, dimly lit office with a tired vinyl couch. To Maris it looked like a princess bed. Ian fished out a blanket from the closet and laid it over her thin shoulders. Before he closed the door, she was asleep.

The air pressure of an impact wrench whining pulled Maris out of her deep sleep. Her neck was stiff and her body ached from sleeping on such a thinly cushioned surface. She walked stiffly out into the garage, where a group of men walked admiringly around the black Mercury. What had been a battered car the night before now looked almost as good as when it had rolled off the showroom floor.

Ian popped the trunk and carried her suitcase into the house behind the body shop where the owner lived. Maris took a hot shower and the owner's wife made her a country breakfast of scrambled eggs, bacon, orange juice and toast. When they had eaten, Ian drove the Mercury to the hotel that Joanne had stayed in for the night, courtesy of the town. They drove down to City Hall, where the Mayor gave Maris the Key to the City. A flash bulb snapped as the photographer got his shots for the local newspaper.

From there the Mercury headed back out to the Interstate with Joanne driving. Ian had been up all night and he immediately fell asleep in the passenger seat as Maris sat quietly in the back seat, watching the scenery go by.

"It's not rock-steady like the Daytona," Joanne observed.

Maris leaned forward and saw Joanne with one finger on the steering wheel.

"Watch," Joanne said as she took her finger off the wheel. The Mercury began to drift to the right. When the car reached the white line, Joanne grasped the wheel with both hands and guided the car back into the lane.

"The car is almost 40 years old, Mom, they probably didn't have time to work on the undercarriage last night," Maris stated defensively.

"Still, not as good as the Daytona," Joanne shot back.

Maris shook her head and rolled her eyes. She opened her mouth but there was nothing she had to say to the woman. Her stomach tightened and she could taste bile in her mouth. "Could you pull over please, I think I am going to be sick," Maris asked breathlessly.

"We are late, just hang your head out the window," Joanne ordered.

Maris unbuckled her seatbelt and leaned toward the driver's side rear window.

"Not this side," Joanne snapped. "I don't want to smell it."

Gasping, Maris lunged for the passenger side. She cranked the tiny window down, hung her head out, and her tight tummy ejected her breakfast. She had held her head out the window as far as she could, but some of the contents of her stomach had trickled down the side of the car. The rest had blown back onto the trunk's lid. Even at 70 MPH, the sun baked the partially digested mess into the paint.

When Joanne stopped two hours later for fuel, Maris did her best to wash the car off. But it was too late – the acid from her stomach had ruined the paint. When she climbed back into the car she glared angrily at the back of Joanne's seat. "At least Rachelle is nice to me," she thought to herself.

Chapter 21

The late afternoon sunlight shimmered off the windows of the black Mercury as it lumbered into the outskirts of Fargo, North Dakota, passing Thunder Road Family Fun Park on the left side of the road. Highway overpasses appeared overhead to say that after a hundred miles of open country, they were returning to civilization.

Ian stirred from a restless slumber in the front seat as Joanne steered the car down the frontage road and pulled into the Motel 6 parking lot. Ian gathered himself together and walked into the office to get them a room. When he returned he directed Joanne around to the back for a place to park. As they unloaded their suitcases from the car, Joanne noticed the West Acres Bowling Alley across the parking lot.

After they were settled into their room, Joanne suggested that they eat dinner and bowl at the bowling alley for Maris' birthday. They walked across the parking lot and made their way through the double doors into the purple-walled alley. The words "Cosmic Bowling" were printed in yellow and scattered periodically along the walls.

They requested their shoes and Joanne ordered a pizza at the snack bar. When Maris went to find herself a bowling ball, Ian shared with the manager that it was her birthday. The manager nodded understandingly as Ian pressed an additional bill into his palm.

In the first game, Joanne racked up a pin count of 180, while Maris accumulated 67. Ian came up with 50. In the second game, Ian recorded a strike on his second frame. He fell to the floor as if he had had a heart attack. Laughing, he reached out his hand for Maris to help him up. Then he pulled her down on top of himself and gave her a kiss on the cheek. "Happy Birthday Baby," he whispered, as they stood up together.

The manager's voice cut through the din. "We would like all of you to join us in wishing Maris Coryell a 'Happy Birthday', as she is joining us all the way from Missouri." Nearly one hundred people stretched across 32 lanes stood and sang a spirited rendition of "Happy Birthday" as a woman appeared with a cake that had 13 candles for Maris to extinguish.

After she blew out the candles, everybody clapped and returned to their games. Maris shared her cake with bowlers on the surrounding lanes. Following the second game, they returned to the motel. Joanne and Maris went to sleep as Ian looked through the phone book.

The next morning the sun cut through their window at the back of the building. Ian was up and ready, as Maris, and then Joanne, took their turns in the bathroom. They walked across 13th Street to Star Mart for breakfast. Maris picked at her food. Ian could tell she was not hungry, and decided that she was stressed at the thought of seeing her own name on a headstone. When he was done eating he excused himself. He went to the motel to get the car.

When he returned Joanne and Maris climbed into the car. He turned onto 13th Street and down two blocks to Sherry's Boutique. As Joanne and Maris climbed out of the car, Ian handed Maris a white paper sack. "You will need this," he offered.

Maris accepted the sack from Ian's hand and looked inside. There was a black clutch purse. She opened it to discover a black pocketbook. She unsnapped the button and found a credit card with her name on it. "Thank you Daddy," she gushed, as she gave him a big hug.

Joanne led Maris inside. A young woman came from behind the counter and politely asked how she could help them. "She needs her first Little Black Dress," Joanne stated curtly.

The young woman nodded understandingly. "One LBD coming up," she cooed. She went through two dress racks and came back with three options.

Ian drove down another block to Country Greenery. He pulled open the front door and strolled across the well-worn wooden floor.

"May I help you?" a woman called from the back.

"I would like to buy some roses," Ian explained.

"How many?"

"Sixty-one."

"Are you going out to Holy Cross Cemetery?"

Ian nodded.

The woman nodded back understandingly. "Rudy, I need five dozen roses," she called over her shoulder as she approached the register.

"Thirty dollars," she stated after she rang up the purchase.

"Shouldn't it be $60?" Ian asked, pointing at the sign.

"Should be," the woman answered matter-of-factly. "That's the '61 special'." She handed him a single rose.

Ian nodded and laid down two $20's on the counter. A lanky teenage boy appeared carrying the 60 roses and followed Ian out to the car, where he laid the flowers in the trunk on top of the sack that contained the laptop computer case. Ian thanked him and slipped him a $5.

"Hooch," Joanne stated when Maris stepped out of the fitting room wearing a dress with black lace that went from her shoulders to her neck. Maris lowered her head and returned to the little room.

"Double Hooch," Joanne proclaimed when Maris reappeared, this time sporting an outfit featuring spaghetti straps.

Joanne said nothing the final time Maris came out, wearing a knee-length dress that covered her shoulders. The saleswoman walked around Maris, tugging it different ways to make sure it fit the girl.

Maris looked at her reflection in the mirror and saw a young lady looking back at her. Her athletic build made her look almost gazelle-like.

The saleswoman agreed that the dress was a good fit. She produced a light blue box and opened it to reveal a pair of black pumps with a tiny heel. Maris slipped them onto her feet and walked back and forth between the women. Joanne said nothing. The saleswoman nodded approvingly.

Maris pulled the credit card out of the pocketbook and the saleswoman processed the transaction. They tossed the clothes Maris had worn into the store into a sack.

When Joanne and Maris walked out of the store, Ian pulled up and they climbed into the car. Ian passed out a cool lemonade to each of them. He pulled back out onto 13th Street, drove west to I-29 and headed North. The black Mercury turned right onto 19th Avenue, drove past North Dakota State University, and took two more turns to arrive on the grounds of Holy Cross Cemetery. Ian stopped at the little brick building and went inside for directions.

He came out and eased the car along the pavement until they could see the top of the black diamond monument, the point standing taller than all the others. Ian picked up the single rose off of the console and pushed open his door. He handed it to Maris as she stepped out. She crossed the pavement and glided across the grass to the Roger Maris gravesite.

She stood there for a moment facing the black diamond, carved with her name. The silhouette of Roger Maris was swinging a bat at the bottom of the diamond with "61 in '61" next to the silhouette. Below that were the words "Against All Odds".

A sob escaped her lips as tears trickled down her cheeks. She sagged to her knees and sniffled. "Are you alright miss?" a male voice asked.

She slowly turned to the figure standing behind her. The sun was behind him so he was almost a shadow. She raised her hand to her forehead to block the sun. "Are you the gardener?" she asked.

He chuckled and ran his hand through his short, cropped hair. "Something like that," he offered. "Why are you crying?"

"That's my name," she said as she pointed at the black diamond. "I have just always thought that he was alive, coaching a Little League team. And someday I would meet a guy and he would say that Roger Maris was his coach and I would tell him my name is Maris and we would get married. Sounds pretty silly, huh?"

"He's still alive as long as you have his name," the man whispered.

Maris looked at the black diamond and wiped her eyes. "Thank you," she whispered as she turned to look at the man again.

He was gone.

Maris stood up to see Ian and Joanne walking toward her. Ian had his arms full of roses.

"Did you see where he went?" Maris asked breathlessly.

"Who?" Ian asked, as he looked around wearily.

"The man I was talking to," Maris answered.

"I didn't see anybody," Ian explained. Joanne shook her head.

Ian busted the wrapping of each of the five dozen roses and laid them in a spray in front of the marker to join the baseballs and golf balls stacked on the base of the marker. He looked closer and saw some coins, two quarters, a dime, and a penny.

"Sixty-one cents," he observed.

Joanne shifted from foot to foot. Ian could tell she was bored. Maris took one final look at the marker and they slowly made their way back to the car.

Nobody spoke as they made their way back down I-29 to West Acres Mall, where the Roger Maris Museum was located. When the Mercury pulled into the parking lot, Joanne's eyes lit up. "That's what I'm talking about," she thought to herself.

They walked into the front door of the mall and studied the directory, then made their way to the museum. Along the way they passed a sportswear store. Maris wanted a shirt that had "Fargo" printed on it, so they went in and purchased one. From there they walked around the corner to see a string of red, white and blue flags along the ceiling chronicling each of Roger Maris' 61 home runs. The glass-enclosed display case included his jerseys, magazine covers, awards, bats, balls and pictures. A monument to him stood in the center of the aisle. It was a lot to take in. Ian pulled out his camera and snapped some pictures.

At the end of the display was a wooden arch that led to an alcove theater with nine seats from Yankee Stadium. From there a person could watch an ongoing tribute movie about Roger Maris. Ian and Maris sat down quietly to watch. Joanne sat down and was soon twitching her legs around.

Driven to distraction, Maris flipped open her clutch purse and dug out the credit card. "Here, go shop," she snapped.

Joanne snatched the card and was gone.

Forty-five minutes later Joanne reappeared with several bags in her hands. Ian sat quietly, reflecting on what he had just seen. Tears trickled down Maris' face as the story ended.

Joanne shook her head and grunted. "I never did understand why he wanted to name you after a dead guy," she grumbled.

"He's not dead!" Maris barked as she stood up from the bleacher seat. "Not as long as I carry his name. And when I have a son I'll name him Roger."

"If you can ever get a man," Joanne chided her as she walked away from the display.

Maris stepped into the wooden archway and raised her middle finger at Joanne's back. Ian's hand appeared on Maris' wrist. Tightening into a vice-like grip, she felt like she was falling in slow motion as she fell against the wooden arch. Her outstretched finger supported her full weight as Ian continued his grip on her wrist. Her finger turned purple and then black.

"Don't EVER do that again!" Ian growled in her face.

Maris opened her mouth to apologize but a gasping whimper was the only sound that came out. A pain shot down through her arm, up her neck, and into her heart. Ian let go and she collapsed to the floor.

Joanne turned around to see Maris struggling to get up using only one arm. "Is she alright?" she asked, oblivious to what had just transpired.

Ian nodded. "Yes, she's overcome with the emotion of the whole day. Well, we better go." He hustled them out of the mall before Security showed up to start asking questions.

Maris, still in her black dress, crawled into the back seat, kicked off her shoes and fell asleep. Joanne looked through her bags of purchases as Ian pointed the Mercury to the West for their next stop at Mount Rushmore.

CHAPTER 22

Pushing through the hilly curves, the black Mercury hung surprisingly well to the road. Maris smiled each time the tires chirped because she knew Ian had taken the big car to its limit.

They had arrived in Rapid City, South Dakota at 2:00am that morning. Ian had found a place to stay, then carried Maris upstairs to their room. He put the "Fargo" shirt on over her little black dress and tucked her into bed. He considered leaving Joanne in the car, but thought better of it and carried her up the stairs and put her into bed as well.

At the bottom of the last hill was the tourist town of Keystone, which featured all manner of Mount Rushmore souvenirs. From there Ian drove the car up the hill to the Mount Rushmore entrance gate and paid to park. They emerged from the car for the short walk across the parking deck through the gray columns. Carved into the top were the words that proclaimed the sight as the Mount Rushmore National Memorial.

They strode upon the gray cobblestone walkway past the Information Center and the bookstore before passing beneath a second colonnade. They turned to the right and stepped into The Carver's Café. Glass walls provided a picturesque view for eating.

They made their way past the bakery to the back where they ordered breakfast. Ian had biscuits and gravy, while Joanne and Maris split the egg skillet. Between bites Maris observed the state flags overhead and took note of the Presidential portraits on the walls.

When they were done eating they continued up the walkway through the Avenue of Flags, where all the states were again represented. It opened up into The Grand Terrace, an expansive viewing area to see Presidents George Washington, Thomas Jefferson, Theodore Roosevelt and Abraham Lincoln carved out of the mountain. They stood there reverently absorbing the view. From there they made their way along the Presidential Trail for a closer look at the mountain, walking along the wooden footpath. Having spent so much time in the car, it was a welcome break to stroll through the wooded area listening to wildlife and breathing in fresh mountain air.

They examined a three-teepee reproduction of a Lakota Indian settlement, looked at a cave-like area, then stepped out onto a wooden platform directly beneath the heads. As they looked almost straight up, a sea of rocks that were bowling ball size and larger stretched up the incline in front of them.

Ian pulled out his camera from the sack he was carrying that he had removed from the trunk and snapped several pictures. Then he pulled the plastic computer case from the sack.

Joanne looked on uncomprehendingly at Ian, not knowing why he would have brought the computer out there. She had been unsuccessful in getting a wireless connection in the mountains. Their eyes locked.

"Détente," Ian stated. "You don't have it and I don't have it." With that he turned and flung the plastic case up onto the rocks.

Joanne watched in stunned disbelief as the case hurtled up into the air onto the rocks and exploded into a rain of plastic chards. Thinking it was the whole computer, she gasped. She turned to Ian, who smirked, daring her to react. Joanne leaped forward like a jaguar and lunged at Ian's throat. Unprepared for the voracity of her response, Ian was caught off guard. She knocked him down onto the wooden platform and wrapped her hands around his throat.

"Stop, you're hurting him!" Maris wailed as she grabbed Joanne's shoulder in an attempt to pry her off of Ian. Joanne grabbed Maris' hand and jerked it away, sending Maris crashing down onto the platform.

The distraction gave Ian the chance he needed. He hinged at the hips, bringing his legs up behind Joanne. He latched his foot under her chin and slammed her head to the platform. With her momentarily dazed, Ian was able to climb out from underneath Joanne. He looked up to see Maris propped up on one knee. Her arm was pulled back like a trip-hammer and her hand was balled up into a fist. He watched breathlessly as his daughter slowly lowered her arm and opened her hand. He was grateful to see that he had raised her well enough that she would not take a cheap shot on a defenseless person.

He picked up Joanne and she punched him in the chest. He deflected the second blow and started to wrestle her back to the car. She cut loose a string of expletives and people began looking at the moving wrestling match.

"It's alright," Ian explained, "She's off her meds." What had seemed to Ian like a short walk now turned into a fight for his life, as Joanne landed two more blows, nearly causing him to lose his grip on her. He dug into his pocket for the car keys and tossed them to Maris.

"Go start the car," he ordered. Maris nodded and ran down the gray walkway with the camera in her hand. By the time they reached the parking lot Ian was completely exhausted. His eye was almost swollen shut and he could taste blood in his mouth. His shirt was ripped to shreds.

Maris had turned the car around, and both doors were open with the seat backs pushed forward. Ian chucked Joanne into the back seat and pushed the driver's seat into place. "There's your precious computer!" Ian snapped as he jumped into the front seat and closed the door. He looked over at Maris as she jumped into the passenger seat and closed her door.

A police siren made a mournful wail off in the distance as Ian pointed the car out onto the street. The police car passed and turned into the Mount Rushmore entrance. Once they were past Keystone, Ian relaxed and looked back at Joanne. She was curled up in the back seat whimpering and caressing the computer. He shook his head and drove to the motel to check out.

There was little talk as Ian drove all night back home. The bug-splattered front end of the black Mercury nosed into the paved lane and climbed up the hill shortly after the sun rose. Completely spent, Ian joined Maris and Joanne in sleep as he nodded off with his seat belt still lashed over his shoulder with the car sitting on the plateau.

Chapter 23

The next morning Ian got up and took the Mercury to the shop for maintenance. The two thousand mile trip had not been kind to the aging car, and attention needed to be paid to all of its operating systems.

Rachelle came up to the shop and took Ian back to her house, as Lacrisha was at school. By mid-morning Joanne was getting prepared to leave the house. "Where are you going?" Maris inquired.

"You are about the nosiest kid in the world," Joanne answered as she looked herself over one more time in the full-length mirror. She climbed into the SRT-8 and left to have an encounter with a guy she met on the Internet.

Maris ordered a pizza to be delivered using her new friend, the credit card, then she worked on finishing the homework she had been given for the trip. After she ate she laid out in the sun for half an hour to work on her tan, then she got up and did some soccer drills to keep her skills sharp. She came inside to get a drink and her eyes fell on the key rack in the kitchen. She drank down the water then lifted the Del Sol key from its peg and walked out onto the plateau where the car was parked outside the garage.

She started the car and cruised down the hill to the street, looking both ways. She saw no cars coming. She crept out onto the highway and drove the car toward the Interstate. At the gas station she lost her nerve. She looked up at Camille's restaurant and turned around in the parking lot. She punched the gas pedal on the way home so she would get back before anyone knew she had been gone. She flew up the driveway and parked on the plateau – nobody was the wiser.

She walked into the garage and looked down to the end where the Daytona sat silently under the faded car cover. She walked down to the winged beast and jerked the cover off the wing -- the rest of the cover fell to the floor like a bridal gown after a wedding.

She pulled open the heavy door and sat down in the ancient leather seat. The big wood-grained steering wheel pleaded with her to stroke it. She ran her hands over the three spokes that led to the center hub and could almost feel the electricity of excitement that pulsated throughout the car. She reached for the key and pressed the clutch and brake pedals to the floor. She turned the key as far as it would go, but nothing happened. She looked up at the dome light and realized that it was not on.

She pulled the hood latch release and climbed out of the car. Standing in front of the behemoth made her appreciate just how massive the car was. She pulled the hood pins and eased the hood up over her head. She looked under the hood and saw that the battery was disconnected. She slipped the connections onto the posts and the interior of the car was bathed in a soft light. She climbed into the front seat and turned the key. The mighty engine cranked over, she pressed the gas to get some fuel up into the carburetor and the engine came to life with a deep heart-like throb.

She let it idle for a little while, watching the temperature gauge climb to a safe level. She pressed the gas pedal and the motor responded with a powerful rumble that filled the garage and rattled the windows. She tapped the pedal again and could feel the warmth of the motor in her heart. She cut off the motor, climbed out of the car and pressed the hood closed. She walked back into the kitchen to get another drink and let the motor cool. Later, she carefully drew up the car cover over the wing and went back inside.

Joanne returned to the house shortly after three o'clock. Bedraggled, she went straight to the bathroom and took a hot bath. Ian returned home with the Mercury shortly thereafter, looking invigorated, like a man who had visited a spa.

Rachelle arrived later with Lacrisha and the girls hugged like long-lost Army buddies. Ian and Rachelle made an attempt at small talk, and Maris could tell immediately where Ian had spent the day – she was glad he was happy.

Joanne emerged from the bathroom and plopped herself down on the couch with the computer in her lap. She made a courtesy wave as Rachelle left the house.

Ian made pasta for dinner. He chimed in from time to time as he and the girls sat at the table discussing the trip. Joanne sat in solitude in the front room, eating and watching a movie.

Later the girls went to Maris' bedroom and Maris told Lacrisha about some of the more unpleasant things about the trip in Spanish. By 10:30pm all the lights in the house were out and all was quiet.

"Are you thirsty?" Maris asked in a hoarse whisper. Lacrisha rolled over and looked up at Maris. She was standing beside the bed wearing the grey Fargo shirt and jeans. Lacrisha closed her eyes and rolled away when she saw that the clock read 1:25am.

Maris touched Lacrisha's shoulder and gently rolled her back over. "Get dressed," she ordered. In a daze Lacrisha climbed out of the bed and slipped into her blouse and slacks. Maris took her hand and led her down the hall, through the kitchen, and past the front room where Joanne was fast asleep. Maris eased the door to the garage open and gently closed it behind them when they were on the steps.

She took Lacrisha's hand and led her over to the Daytona. In one swift move she whipped off the car cover to expose the car to the moonlight cascading through the garage window. Lacrisha gasped at the enormity of the car.

"It's huge," she whispered.

Maris smiled as she unlatched the garage door and quietly lifted it up on its rails. The cool night air breathed across their young faces.

"Help me push," Maris whispered after she pulled the shifter into neutral and stepped to the front of the car.

Lacrisha hesitated. This did not look to her like it was going to end well.

Maris stood up and looked at her friend, rooted in place. "What?"

"This is crazy."

"Are you going to quit on me too?" Maris snapped.

Lacrisha lowered her head. "I won't quit on you," she whispered. She stepped to the front of the car and together they were able to push it out onto the plateau under the starry night.

Lacrisha went to the back of the car while Maris went to the driver's door to push and steer. As soon as the car was rolling she jumped in and closed the door. She turned the key to the "run" position, pushed the shifter into second gear, and let out on the clutch. The mighty engine sputtered to life halfway down the lane. Maris applied the brakes, and Lacrisha ran up to the car and climbed into the passenger seat.

"Fancy meeting you in a place like this," Maris quipped as she eased the car down to the highway. She flicked on the headlights and pulled out, the big motor throbbing like a heartbeat in her ears. She rolled down the window and the breeze teased her hair. She smiled – she was free.

They rumbled past Camille's and the gas station, without hesitation this time. Maris pointed the car up the ramp and they were out on the Interstate. She eased the shifter through the gear box and they were doing 100 MPH when they blew past a sedan parked on the side of the road. For a moment she thought it was a squad car and her stomach did a flip. But no lights came on and the car did not give chase.

At the next exit she took the ramp off the Interstate, drove under the overpass and went back up the ramp on the other side. Just past the ramp they passed another sedan sitting on the side of the road. She began to wonder, as she flew back to her exit. She guided the car down the ramp, under the overpass and into the gas station.

"Thirsty?" Maris asked her ghost-white friend. Lacrisha nodded. The girls got out of the car and walked inside.

A balding man doing a crossword puzzle looked up from behind the counter and nodded, then did a double-take when he saw how young the girls were. His eye caught sight of the Daytona and his jaw dropped. Maris smiled and nodded back as she led Lacrisha to the soda fountain, where they each poured themselves a drink.

They walked up to the counter to pay. "Five dollars on pump five," Maris stated as she handed the man her credit card. He took the card and nodded. He ran it through the machine and handed it back to her.

"Thank you," she said with a smile. She took a sip of her drink and led Lacrisha out the door. Outside she pumped the five dollars of gas into the car so the gas gauge would not betray her trip. They climbed back into the car. With the cup between her legs, she tried to maneuver the elongated vehicle past the gas pumps and grazed the front bumper against one of the concrete posts that protected the pumps.

Both girls gasped, they jumped out of the car and ran to the front. A red smudge the size of a palm had appeared on the front driver's side of the nose cone. Maris dropped her drink and ran over to the windshield washer container on the post. She raced back and tried to wash the smudge. It faded a little.

Her tummy tightened as she trudged back to return the brush to its container. She walked back to Lacrisha, who had squatted in front of the car.

"My mom has had this happen once, it ought to buff right out," Lacrisha offered.

"Hopefully," Maris breathed as she climbed back into the car and headed for home.

Getting to the driveway seemed to take forever. She cut off the headlights at the bottom of the hill and drove up using the Moon as a guide. When she reached the plateau she turned off the engine as they coasted to the garage door. Maris got out and began to lift the door. When it reached her knees, she could see lights flashing on the floor. She eased it the rest of the way up and discovered a squad car backed into the garage. A policeman and Ian were sitting in the front seat. Ian smiled and waved.

Behind her, six more squad cars roared down the highway and charged up the lane, coming to a stop on the hill. Several officers piled out and Ian and the officer that was in the garage were standing on the plateau. "Thanks to all of you," Ian sighed as he handed the gold badge to the policeman from the garage.

"How did you know?" Maris asked.

"I'm a dad, that's what I do," Ian stated. "When I heard you leave I contacted the Colonel and he had the roads blocked off so you would not get chased and nothing would happen to you."

"So you have to give up the badge for me?" she cried.

"Yep, this is my last free one."

"I am sorry Daddy," she whimpered. "I didn't mean to."

"It's alright Baby, you're home."

The kitchen door opened and Joanne walked out wearing sweatpants and a T-shirt. "What's going on?" she snapped. Then she saw the Daytona outside the garage.

"What is going on!" she demanded. She raced outside and walked around the car looking for any damage. When she got to the front of the car she discovered the smudge.

"Are you crazy!" she shrieked.

"If I am I got it from you!" Maris bellowed back.

Joanne slapped Maris' mouth with the back of her hand. Maris reeled and caught herself before she fell. She charged Joanne, knocking her to the ground. A beefy policeman peeled Maris off of Joanne. Maris kicked him in the groin, the policeman let her go and Maris pounced on Joanne again.

This time three policemen grabbed Maris and pulled her off. She trashed around like a fish caught in a net, dislocating her shoulder in the process. The Colonel walked up and gave her a low-dose taser and she quit thrashing. The Colonel pulled his handcuffs off his belt and clicked them around Maris' wrists. One of the officers led her to the back of the squad car and pushed her inside.

"Assaulting an officer usually results in doing some time," the Colonel stated to Ian matter-of-factly.

Ian nodded as he watched two officers help Joanne to her feet and dust her off.

"Are you going to be able to take care of this?" the Colonel asked, looking Ian in the eye.

Ian nodded sheepishly. "I got it," he whispered.

The Colonel went back to the squad car where Maris sat and explained what charges she would have been facing and concluded by telling her to straighten up. Maris nodded and the Colonel unlocked the handcuffs. She limped past Lacrisha on her way to the house and whispered that she was sorry as she followed Ian and Joanne into the house.

Lacrisha climbed into the Colonel's car and he drove her home to an unhappy Rachelle, whom Ian had called to let her know that Lacrisha was on her way.

Maris did not fall asleep until dawn. By then Ian had buffed the smudge off the Daytona's bumper. Satisfied, Joanne went back to sleep on the couch.

When Maris did awaken around 10:00am, Ian was in the kitchen making breakfast. The girl slipped quietly into her chair at the table and looked up expectantly at her father.

"I'm just glad you are home Baby."

"Me too," she whispered.

When Joanne awakened she took a shower and ate breakfast leftovers. She went into the bedroom and gathered up all her clothes that she could fit into the backseat and trunk of the Daytona, then drove away without saying a word.

A week later, when Ian and Maris were not there, Joanne came back to get the rest of her things and packed them into the SRT-8, and she was gone.

When Ian and Maris returned they saw that Joanne's things were gone. Maris did not even cry. She was relieved. Ian sighed with relief and called Rachelle to invite her and Lacrisha over for their first dinner as a family.

CHAPTER 24

In December the four of them flew commercial to a resort in Mexico for a combination Christmas vacation-honeymoon. They rode ATV's through the jungle, snorkeled, and hit every buffet they encountered. Maris and Lacrisha were able to use their Spanish to talk to all of the resort workers. They met two brothers from Baltimore, Maryland by the names of Johnny and Cal. They became fast friends and joined them frequently for meals. Ian took the boys fishing one day to get to know them better.

When they left the resort to go their separate ways, promises were made to phone call, text, and instant-message each other. The long-distance relationships were just fine with Ian.

For Maris' 14th birthday the plan was to return to the May Day Car Show. They took the crimson Lincoln and pulled into the gas station for a fill-up. They all went inside as Ian paid. On the way out Maris stopped in her tracks, and Ian almost tripped over her. He looked where her eyes were focused and saw a classic cars sale magazine. On the cover was a white Dodge Charger Daytona with an orange Scat Pack stripe.

"Can I get it?" Maris asked hopefully.

"The magazine or the car?" Ian asked, unsure of what she was talking about.

"The magazine," she answered quietly.

Ian nodded and Maris went back to the counter and paid with her credit card. They all trooped out to the Lincoln and climbed inside the car. Maris read the advertisement aloud, and the VIN number indicated that it was Joanne's car.

"It says it has a new clutch – do you think I messed it up?" she asked somberly.

Ian laughed heartily. "No Baby, when I pulled it into the garage it was fine."

"That phone number is a California number," Rachelle offered. "In the Valley I think." It was quiet in the car for several minutes.

"Could we get the car?" Maris asked meekly.

"Why do you want that?" Ian demanded.

"Well, when Joanne gets better we could give it back to her," Maris suggested hopefully.

Ian shook his head. Rachelle smiled at the young girl's optimism.

"How are you going to take care of that?" Ian inquired, as she did not have a job. Maris and Lacrisha put their heads together and whispered to each other in Spanish.

"We could give children Spanish lessons," Maris proposed. "And Japanese."

Ian eased the car to a stop at a light. "We'll see," he breathed.

When they arrived at the show they found their spot and Ian rolled the convertible top back. The girls went off to look at the cars. Rachelle went to go get some drinks, talking on her cell phone as she walked. When she returned she was smiling as she handed Ian a drink.

"We got it," she announced.

"How are we going to afford that?" Ian demanded.

"I called the studio and they are going to put out a boxed set of the television show I was on – we go out there next week for a promotional shoot, get the car, and drive home."

"We?" Ian inquired.

"All of us, the girls can be my #1 fans."

"I thought I was your #1 fan," Ian cooed as he held her close and kissed her. "Thank you for doing this for my daughter."

"Correction, our daughter," Rachelle stated.

Ian nodded.

"Hey there Ian," a man's voice called. Ian turned to see an older man walking toward him wearing a green windbreaker, then he saw the "Ghostbusters" emblem peeking out from the partially buttoned jacket and realized that it was the doctor who had raced them to the hospital all those years ago. Ian introduced Rachelle to the man and they had a good laugh.

Maris and Lacrisha reappeared, Ian introduced the doctor and Maris gave him a hug and thanked him for the ride. They all talked for a few minutes then the doctor asked to speak to Ian alone. They walked up a line of Corvettes.

"I saw Joanne," the doctor began.

"Oh really, how is she doing?" Ian politely asked.

The doctor pulled a plastic bag out of his pocket and handed it over. Ian unwrapped the bag and pulled out a thin plastic box. He saw that it was a DVD. Joanne was on the cover, her hair was cut short and bleached blond. Her face featured a "come hither" look, she was wearing a slinky red dress and had a tribal tattoo around her bicep.

Ian blanched, he flipped it over and glanced at the pictures on the back. Then he looked up at the doctor.

"Just thought I would let you know," the doctor explained. He turned and melted into the crowd.

Ian busted the DVD in half and threw it into a garbage can. "What was that?" Maris asked lightly as she walked up and took her dad's hand into her hand.

"Trash," Ian answered as they went back to the Lincoln.

All four of them flew commercial to Los Angeles, where the studio sent a long black limousine to pick them up and they rode out to Burbank. They ate at the studio commissary, then Rachelle, Lacrisha and Maris went to wardrobe for their fittings.

At two o'clock they walked out onto a stage in front of a recreated set from the television show and announced the release of the boxed set of DVD's. Cameras flashed as Rachelle talked. When asked why now, she explained that it was the right time.

After half an hour of questions they descended from the stage and Rachelle signed autographs for an hour. Eventually a studio employee stepped in and freed Rachelle from the fans. A studio executive showed up and gave her a hug as he thanked her. She told him she would think about the movie offer.

From there they all four climbed into the Daytona, which the studio had purchased, and security escorted them to the front gate. Ian eased the big Dodge out onto the street and pointed it to the East.

Two days later they wheeled into the Rapid City, South Dakota airport to pick up Johnny and Cal, who had flown out to join them. They found a hotel and went swimming during the afternoon. After dinner they played miniature golf and saw the pig races at one of the attractions surrounding Mount Rushmore.

The next morning they got up and went to Mount Rushmore for breakfast in the Carver's Café. This trip was at a much more leisurely pace. They were able to see the sights and take the tour. From there they made their way over to where the Crazy Horse Memorial was being cut out of another mountain. They had lunch there and paid the extra fee to ride up to where the face was located and have their picture taken.

Eventually they returned Johnny and Cal to the airport for their departure, hugs were exchanged and the young men boarded their plane for their lonely flight home without their dear friends. The four of them returned to the hotel and had a late dinner before going to bed. The next morning they awoke and partook of the complimentary Continental breakfast then headed out to the Daytona for the 15-hour drive home. Along the way, on some of the back roads, Ian let Maris drive close to 100 miles. When they arrived home that night everyone was happy to sleep in their own beds.

The next morning in the front room Maris and Lacrisha were working on the words to use for their newspaper advertisement for language lessons. Rachelle was listening from the kitchen. She walked into the front room.

"How would you like to work with me this Summer?" she asked casually.

The girls looked up at her questioningly. "Doing what?" they asked in unison.

"Oh, I don't know, make a movie maybe."

"Yes!" the girls screamed as they jumped off the couch, almost knocking Rachelle to the floor.

"Make-up!" Rachelle called out, like she was on the set ready to shoot a scene. She wrapped her arms around the girls. It was going to be a fun summer, if she could just get over the nauseous feeling she had been experiencing lately.